THE WOMAN'S COMFORT BOOK

ALSO BY JENNIFER LOUDEN

The Pregnant Woman's Comfort Book
The Couple's Comfort Book
The Woman's Retreat Book
Comfort Secrets for Busy Women

The Woman's Comfort Book

A Self-Nurturing Guide for Restoring Balance in Your Life

Jennifer Louden

HarperOne
An Imprint of HarperCollins*Publishers*

HarperOne

THE WOMAN'S COMFORT BOOK: *A Self-Nurturing Guide for Restoring Balance in Your Life.*

Library of Congress Cataloging-in-Publication Data

Louden, Jennifer.
The woman's comfort book : a self-nurturing guide for restoring balance in your life / Jennifer Louden.
p. cm.
Includes bibliographical references.
ISBN 978-0-06-077667-1
1. Women—Psychology. 2. Nurturing behavior. 3. Self-care, Health. 4. Self-help techniques. I. Title.
HQ1206.L68 1992
646.7'0082—dc20 91-55316
CIP

15 RRD(H) 10

For
Betty Marie Louden,
my mother

CONTENTS

FOREWORD

Until a few years ago, I felt like a fake. I had written five books about self-care and living life from the inside out, and yet I still handled deadlines like a drama queen, got burned out, ate unconsciously, wondered if I was living my life purpose, and otherwise failed to honor and listen to my inner wisdom—not just once in a while but sometimes *daily*. I forgot to ask myself mindful questions. I forgot to meditate. I avoided yoga, preferring to be a giant head, unattached to a body with sensations and desires. Yet the more I demanded perfection from myself, the more disconnected I became. What I have since learned—and must find ways to remind myself of every day—is that the part of me, the part of you, that is compelled to read, write, confabulate, teach, quest, coach, and learn is not the part that demands perfection in all things. The part of us that quests is the part of us that loves our imperfections; it is the part of us that knows our deepest strengths *are* our imperfections.

Or as the fourteenth-century Sufi master and poet Hafiz wrote, "Now is the season to know / That everything you do / Is sacred."

Self-care is radical; it changes lives. When we practice self-care, we start refusing to stay in relationships, jobs, and attitudes that depend upon our hating ourselves. We begin to see possibilities where before there were only habits. "I was in bed early because I had a terrible flu," Manuela said, recalling about her self-care discovery. "There are these lines in your book about taking a close look at your body, become friends with your body. I was too weak to get up, so I looked at my hands. It was as if I had never seen these hands before. I had put on nail polish maybe a thousand times, but I had never taken a real look at my hands. I stared for what might have been many hours—they were like the hands of a stranger. I was shocked to find I had treated not only my hands but my whole body this way. Dressing it up, making it look nice, keeping it in shape but only so I could make it attractive to others. I had never looked at my body as a 'part' of me, as something that is mine. I was very rattled by this experience, but it began my year of awakening. I left a bad relationship, quit my job, and moved to the city in which I had always dreamed of living. It was the beginning of my adult life!"

We read Manuela's story and we think, "Yes!" Yet I've heard from so many women over the years that self-care is a good idea but only possible if you have a certain amount of time or money. That is a story we tell ourselves when we are still trapped in putting ourselves last.

"I have an autistic daughter who will be twelve in February," wrote Lisa in an email. "She is still in diapers, needs to be fed, and does not talk. My husband has hepatitis C, and my dad is not well. I take everybody to the doctor often. I don't have time for myself, yet I started a journal to learn who I am and what I want and need out of life. I lost your book, bought it again, and am currently working through it for a second time. My husband mentioned he likes me better when I am reading it and working in my journal! I have learned what 'inner spiritual happiness' is for me, and I cherish it."

Diane was misdiagnosed at seventeen as a schizophrenic and spent the next twenty years in and out of hospitals. Then she found Gina, a psychotherapist, who was finally able to diagnose her correctly and help her get treatment—treatment that included "learning I had a 'right' to be gentle and forgiving of myself. Gina told me my first move was to buy *The Woman's Comfort Book*. By reading it and attempting to follow the exercises, I finally got to the point where I knew I *deserved* my humanity; it was okay to comfort myself. The first week out of the hospital, I pitched a 'tent' in my bedroom and took long, warm candle-lit baths to reduce my anxiety. Healing is possible, and caring about yourself isn't an 'indulgence.' It's a basic human right." Amen Diane and Lisa.

In the twelve years since *The Woman's Comfort Book* was published—not to mention the three years before in which I began my personal search to articulate what self-care is—people across the world have become more candid, more voracious, more curious, and more furious about creating days, weeks, and lives that fit. In a small town in Indiana and a bank board room in Germany, a flat in Dublin, a farm in Australia, an apartment in Switzerland, in Japan, Brazil, and Sweden, we are stepping out of lives that bind, pinch, and creep and into lives that soar, flow, and float. While it is not necessarily becoming easier to make these moves, now there is a growing cultural conversation supporting us as we feel our way into a more gentle and whole way of living. We don't feel so alone when we turn away from endless striving and the endless more, more, more and turn toward listening to our inner guidance.

We read these women's stories, and we know we are not alone. We are each, in our own way, building a solid and dependable relationship with the one person we can count on no matter what—ourselves. More and more women—and men—are doing this: creating lives that fit, creating lives that matter. You are one of them.

Welcome to the revolution.

Jennifer Louden
November 2003
Bainbridge Island, Washington

INTRODUCTION:
How to Read This Book

It's pouring, you had a miserable day at work, you got stuck in a traffic jam, and the only message on the answering machine is a wrong number.

or

You're late picking up the kids from day care, you've got a splitting headache, the paper grocery bag splits as you walk to the front door, and you can't remember the last time you had any time to yourself.

or

You're exhausted, but you won't take time off because everyone is counting on you. The phone rings, you agree to volunteer for another community fund-raiser, but as you reach to hang up, your back goes out and you end up in bed for a week.

or

All your friends are out of town, you haven't had a decent date in months, your roommate ate the last piece of pizza, there's nothing on TV, and you don't feel like reading. . . .

Now, what do you do?

A. Buy a gallon of double chocolate chip ice cream and eat the whole thing?

B. Call your mother, who will tell you to stop whining, which will only make you feel worse?

C. Sleep for a month?

D. Pick up *The Woman's Comfort Book: A Self-Nurturing Guide for Restoring Balance in Your Life*?

Why Nurture Ourselves?

Because self-nurturing is vital. Women take care of others every day. But how often do we turn our wonderful nurturing ability toward ourselves?

Self-care is essential for our survival; it is essential as the basis for healthy, authentic relationships; it is essential if we honestly want to nurture the people we care about.

Self-care is not selfish or self-indulgent. We cannot nurture others from a dry well. We need to take care of our own needs first, then we can give from our surplus, our abundance. When we nurture others from a place of fullness, we feel renewed instead of taken advantage of. And they feel renewed too, instead of guilty. We have something precious to give others when we have been comforting and caring for ourselves and building up self-love.

Why We Don't Take Care of Ourselves

The synonyms in my thesaurus for nurturing are *female*, *feminine*, *gentle*, *ladylike*, *tender*, and *womanly!* As women, we are taught to meet everyone else's needs before we nurture ourselves. And as we are groomed into compliant beings, we come to believe that the people in our lives will anticipate and meet our needs as we do theirs. When this does not happen, we begin to feel we have no right to our needs and desires. Add to this the fact that as women we have not traditionally been taught to care for our self-esteem or to value ourselves as independent, worthwhile people. What we end up with is women who are experts at nurturing others—until we drop of exhaustion or illness or escape into excessive drinking, shopping, or eating. We are goaded into devaluing self-nurturing. We either end up believing we don't deserve self-care or, if we do, that it must be the last thing on our mighty list of Things to Do.

Defining Comfort and Self-Nurturing

I define *comfort* for the purpose of this book as that warm, safe feeling you get from lying in bed watching the rain fall, knowing you don't have to go out of the house if you don't want to. Comfort is also that vital, connected feeling you get when you talk openly with your partner or a close friend. Comfort is a place to fortify yourself for upcoming or ongoing struggles and for the challenge of inner work.

I define *self-nurturing* as having the courage to pay attention to your needs. Nurturing also means empowerment, the power that comes when you stretch and fulfill a goal. And finally, nurturing is celebration, taking the time to applaud being alive, being you.

Above all, I define *nurturing* and *comfort* as self-acceptance. When we finally learn that self-care begins and ends with ourselves, we no longer demand sustenance and happiness from others for our well-being. In healthy self-care, we can find the freedom to choose and direct our own lives, and that is nurturing indeed.

Why I Wrote the Book

Four years ago I thought my life had fallen apart. The crumbling started with a skiing accident. In the two years that followed, I battled depression, a creative block the size of Texas, and my body's rebelling against me. I broke up with my partner of five years. I sold my house and moved into a six-hundred-square-foot guest house owned by nice people who drove me immediately crazy. My dog bit me. I lost the money I had made on my house in the stock market crash. I wrecked my car. My uncle died. But worst of all, I couldn't write. My slim career as a screenwriter faded away.

My life ground to a halt. I could barely function. But that didn't stop me from running a constant litany of self-hate and regret in my mind, while I continued to try to write. I thought I was being brave, pulling myself up by my bootstraps.

I sought counseling and was advised to stop writing. The idea came as such a shock that I remember thinking, "This woman is crazy!" But a few days later, still miserable and not writing, my leg in a brace, I decided to heed her advice. Suddenly I felt a weight lift from my shoulders, and a title, *The Woman's Comfort Book*, popped into my head.

I now realize that ceasing to write was the most self-nurturing thing I could do. A large part of my problems, culminating in my inability to write, was the result of my putting all my effort into external achievement and placing no importance on caring for myself. I needed to trust what my inner voice was telling me, which was to slow down, take some time to care for me. But I felt too guilty about not being ambitious to heed my intuition. And so a dangerous prison formed: I couldn't take time to care for myself because I felt I should keep working, but I couldn't write because I wasn't nurturing myself. What a mess!

I began to learn (very, very slowly) the primary importance of self-nurturing. I read everything I could find on the subject. I experimented with journal exercises, art therapy, bodywork, Native American ritual, and hypnotherapy. I interviewed women I heard about who were exceptional at caring for themselves. I mailed hundreds of questionnaires to women around the world, asking what they did for comfort. I continued in therapy, which remains one of the best moves I've ever made. I began to realize many, many women are in my shoes. We all need, for a wide variety of reasons, to learn to nurture ourselves, but we have little support and limited ideas on how to accomplish this.

Over the course of five years, I have learned how to integrate self-nurturing into my life. That doesn't mean I have mastered the art. Self-care remains a challenge, but an extremely enriching one. I have put this book together as a way to share what I have learned, and I conduct workshops for other women struggling with self-nurturing.

How to Use *The Woman's Comfort Book*

This is a reference book. It suggests things to do instead of telling you why you should do them. You don't need to read it all in one sitting. References to other chapters appear in the margins because many of the chapters are interrelated. For example, "Sweet Scents" and "Herbal Help" contain bathing recipes you can use in "Bathing Pleasures." In "Heal Your Habitat" you will find ideas for simplifying your environment, and in "Simplify" there are ideas for simplifying other areas of your life.

Flip through the book. Read what interests you, what comforts you. Or refer to the chart in the middle of the book for a list of chapters that relate to whatever ails you. I hope you find enough range here to help you in many different moods and at many different times in your life. Maybe something that seems silly or too involved now will appeal to you later. Ultimately, comfort is a very personal experience. My hope is this book will provide inspiration for your personal exploration of what is comforting and nurturing to *you*.

ABOUT RELAXING

Throughout the book you will see the word *relax* like this:

Relax.

I have used it as a kind of shorthand for the meditations throughout the book so you won't have to reread the same relaxation instructions over and over. When you see **relax,** refer back to this chapter for help, or relax in any manner that works for you.

Most of the meditations in this book are short enough for you to read through, then close your eyes and recall. But a few longer guided visualizations are included. The best thing to do with these is to read them into a tape recorder, leaving appropriate pauses where you imagine you will need a little more time. Try playing music in the background while you record.

Relax

Lie down someplace quiet. Close your eyes. Take a deep breath. Hold it for a moment. Slowly let it out. Inhale. Imagine you are breathing pure relaxation in. Hold your breath. Now exhale, and imagine you are breathing out all the tension of your day, your week, your life. Do this a few more times.

Check your body. Are there areas of tension? Inhale, and send your breath of pure relaxation to the tense area. Imagine your breath curling around the knotted muscle, the stored stress. Exhale sharply, expelling every bit of tension from this area. Do this to all other tense areas in your body. Take all the time you need. Now, imagine someone is giving you a gentle massage. The hands touching you are full of love. You are now filled with a deep and wonderful inner calm, and you are ready for whatever you want to do next.

CHECKING YOUR BASIC NEEDS

What Is It?

A need is something we require for our well-being, like food, sunlight, contact with other humans; our needs should be nonnegotiable, things we cannot do without. But sometimes we get so wrapped up in life, in surviving, in getting ahead, in taking care of others, we lose sight of these basic requirements. Don't let that happen! Healthy self-care begins with checking to see if you are meeting your basic needs and then working to fulfill them.

You'll Need:

A pencil.

When to Do This:

- When you are vaguely dissatisfied, depressed, or tense.
- When you can't remember the last time you got a good night's sleep, relaxed, or ate a healthy meal.

What to Do:

Checklist

This list will help you create a picture of your lifestyle. Check off the needs you are meeting regularly.

_____ Do you usually get six to eight hours of sleep?

_____ Do you eat something fresh and unprocessed every day?

_____ Do you allow time in your week to touch nature, no matter how briefly?

_____ Do you get enough sunlight, especially in the wintertime?

_____ Do you drink enough water?

_____ Do you see your gynecologist (or the equivalent) at least once a year?

_____ Do you see a dentist every six months?

Checklist *A good question*

_____ Do you know enough about your body and health needs?

_____ Do you get regular sexual thrills?

_____ Do you feel you get enough *fun* exercise?

_____ Are you hugged and touched amply?

_____ Do you make time for friendship? Do you nurture your friendships?

_____ Do you have friends you can call when you are down, friends who really listen?

_____ Can you honestly ask for help when you need it?

_____ Do you regularly release your negative emotions?

_____ Do you forgive yourself when you make a mistake?

_____ Do you do things that give you a sense of fulfillment, joy, and purpose?

_____ Is there abundant beauty in your life? Do you allow yourself to see beauty and to bring beauty into your home and office?

_____ Do you make time for solitude?

_____ Are you getting daily or weekly spiritual nourishment?

_____ Can you remember the last time you laughed until you cried?

_____ Do you ever accept yourself for who you are?

These questions are not meant to make you feel bad or guilty. They are only meant as kind reminders to help you see how you are currently caring for yourself.

Checking Your Basic Needs

See "When I Think of Comfort, I Think of Food: Truly Comfort Yourself"; "Money, Money, Money: Inherit from Your Intuition"; "The Shadow Side of Comfort: Mindful Comfort"; and "Simplify: Three Good Questions" for more help activating your inner voice.

A Good Question

Get in the habit of asking yourself, as often as possible, this magic question:

> What do I need to help me better care for myself right now?

Slow down whenever you feel tense, strange, or rotten, and take a minute to consider the question. This process will help activate your intuition and speed you toward developing a range of ways to nurture yourself more deeply.

RESOURCES:

Too Good for Her Own Good, by Claudia Bepko and Jo-Ann Krestan (Harper & Row, 1990). Very helpful book about self-nurturing and how it relates to the feminine mandate of being good.

Women's Bodies, Women's Wisdom: Creating Physical and Emotional Health, by Christiane Northrup (Bantam Books, 1995). Think of it as a more empowering and holistic *Our Bodies, Ourselves*.

The Wisdom of Menopause, by Christiane Northrup (Doubleday, 2003). Extremely comprehensive although sometimes a bit overwhelming.

Start Where You Are: A Guide to Compassionate Living, by Pema Chodron (Shambhala, 2001). No need to wait for things to change to start creating more inner peace and wisdom.

The Intimacy and Solitude Workbook, by Stephanie Dowrick (Norton, 1996). A phenomenally powerful workbook about finding yourself while still being in a relationship.

Breathing: The Master Key to Self-Healing, by Andrew Weil, M.D. (Sounds True, 1999). One of the best relaxation/consciousness tapes that is also widely available.

COMFORT JOURNAL

What Is It?

Remember rainy days when you were young? Coloring books spread across the kitchen table or watercolors washed across paper? Or perhaps you liked to make up stories? Lost in your imagination, the rain beating a soft rhythm on the roof, you could spend hours playing.

A comfort journal is a safe place where you can doodle, compose, paste, and jot anything that relates to your ideas of self-nurturing. It is a place where you can lose yourself in creating your personal sourcebook of comfort. You will be comforted when you work in it and comforted when you look back through it.

A comfort journal is not about art, perfection, or genius. Making a comfort journal is about doing what pleases *you*, what helps you feel playful and free. Immerse yourself in the process of discovery!

You'll Need:

Your wonderful, boundless imagination.

Any of the supplies listed below under "Creative Tools."

When to Do It:

- When you feel the need to lose yourself in creative activity for its own sake.
- When the part of you that is still a child wants to get messy.
- When you are exploring what is comforting to you.
- When you are crabby or restless.

What to Do:

Creative Tools

Following is a big list intended to jog your creative side. Please don't think you need to spend a lot of money. Look around your house. Clean out drawers. When you are buying art supplies for your kids, buy some for yourself too.

Creative tools
Investigate what being good to yourself means
A collage of comforting images
Joy list
Free associations
Done list
Love list
Doodle the blues away
A comforting scene
Clips

- An eight-by-twelve sketch book with a durable cover or an eight-by-twelve spiral notebook with drawing paper and pocket folders for odds and ends.
- Colored cellophane. Clay. Crayons, Cray-Pas, fluorescent Crayolas.
- Fabric scraps. Felt. Feathers. Flowers.
- Glue. Glue sticks work great too.
- Leaves. Letters. Bring out comforting letters and photocopy them.
- Magazines. Clip pictures that appeal to you. Store them in a basket or folder. Old greeting cards and old photographs are valuable too. Markers. All colors. Metallic anything—glitter, confetti, pens, foil.
- Paints of all kinds. Try metallic colors. What about finger paints and watercolors? Paintbrushes, toothbrushes, Q-tips, sponges. Paper. Paper scraps, wrapping paper, wallpaper, shelf paper, construction paper, poster board. Pencils. Colored pencils. Play-Doh. Ribbons. Rubber stamps.
- String. Shells. Scissors.
- Yarn.

Put some thought into where you store your comfort journal. You must feel that you can write or draw anything you like in your journal without fear of anyone else reading it.

Investigate What Being Good to Yourself Means

Place your comfort journal and a pen nearby. Close your eyes and concentrate on your breathing for a moment. Reflect on the phrase "being good to myself." When you are ready, take up your pen and list *everything* that comes to mind. Don't worry if it doesn't make sense or if it's just a fragment of a thought. Pour your impressions of what being good to yourself means into your journal.

Put this list away for a few days to allow yourself time to gain some objectivity. When you are ready, read over your list. What insights can you glean?

Take ten minutes to write about what you discover. Try to avoid being judgmental. Now, based on your observations, devise five new comfort activities, and do them in the next week.

See "A Self-Care Schedule: Register Your Rapture" for help scheduling.

A Collage of Comforting Images

Clip appealing pictures from magazines, photocopy happy photographs of friends and family, add keepsakes from good times. Play with the images like a puzzle, striving to create connections with your inner self. See what you can learn about yourself and comfort.

See "A Personal Sanctuary: A Comfort Box."

Joy List

Make a list of one hundred things that make you happy—warm, peaceful things that create a sense of joy and well-being in your life. Record tangible items, like five dollars found in your pocket, and intangible things, like a smile from a stranger. Include things as personal as sweaty sex and as obvious as chocolate chip cookies. Add to this list weekly. Read this list when you're blue.

Free Associations

Pick one word and let your mind run with it. Try *nurture*, *comfort*, *well-being*, *relaxation*, *support*, and *create*. Write down all the words, phrases, and ideas that pop into your mind, or create a sculpture or drawing from your associations.

Done List

A good exercise to do before bed.

See "Comfort Rituals: Going-to-Sleep Ritual."

Write down everything that you accomplished today. Instead of a "to do" list, this is a "done" list. Include everything!

Walked the dog

Called the plumber

Made it through a tough day at the office

Exercised

Drank lots of water

Didn't yell at the kids when they forgot to water the lawn

Give yourself credit for what you did instead of what you didn't do. Own all your successes.

Love List

Write down everything you love about yourself. Get specific. For example, the shape of your shoulder or the way you sneeze; how you run your business or love your children; your talent for dancing or your penchant for reading. Reread this list when you're loathing yourself.

Doodle the Blues Away

When you need to be comforted but don't know what to do, close your eyes and doodle. Let your feelings flow through the pen or paintbrush. Let all your emotions course down your arm and out of your body. Empty yourself.

A Comforting Scene

Draw, sketch, or paint a comforting scene. It can be any place or activity you want. Make your scene as personal as you can. You might sketch the outside of your house in winter, with light shining from the windows. Or select a picture of your family, color it, and add important symbols. Or paint a tropical beach with your lover on it, basking in the sun. Draw whatever makes you feel sensations of comfort, reassurance, security, and safety.

Clips

Thumb through magazines until a comforting picture, wise quote, or article about an exotic place leaps out at you. Clip and paste this in your comfort journal, then write about whatever these images or words conjure up for you.

RESOURCES:

Writing Down the Bones, by Natalie Goldberg (Shambhala, 1986), and *Wild Mind*, by Natalie Goldberg (Bantam Books, 1990). Wonderful books that advocate using writing as a means of moving deeper into your life.

The Well-Being Journal, by Lucia Capacchione (Newcastle, 1989). Could be subtitled "A Self-Care Journal."

Comfort Secrets for Busy Women, by Jennifer Louden (Source Books, 2003). The follow-up to this book, ten years later. Meet the Comfort Queen.

SoulCollage: An Intuitive Collage Process for Individuals and Groups, by Seena B. Frost (Hanford Mead Publishers, 2001).

The Nine Modern Day Muses: Ten Guides to Creative Inspiration for Artists, Poets, Lovers, and Other Mortals Wanting to Live a Dazzling Existence, by Jill Baldwin Badonsky (Gotham, 2003). A playful book chock-full of ways to jump-start your creativity.

Pencil Dancing, by Mari Messer (Walking Stick Press, 2001). Hundreds of creative prompts to get your writing flowing while your inner critic stays silent.

The Twelve Secrets of Highly Creative Women, by Gail McMeekin (Red Wheel/Weiser, 2000). A fascinating and inspiring examination of highly creative women in different disciplines.

The Creative Habit: Learn It and Use It for Life, by Twyla Tharp (Simon and Schuster, 2003). The legendary choregrapher shares her personal creativity practices.

Websites:

Comfort Queen—see the Inner Organizer feature
http://www.comfortqueen.com

Intensive Journal
http://www.intensivejournal.org

Joyce Chapman
http://www.joycechapman.com

A SELF-CARE SCHEDULE

What Is It?

The most basic and precious tenet of self-nurturing is to take time for yourself. *(Time? I'm too busy. Where am I going to find time for me?)* The vicious cycle clicks in: you are too busy to nurture yourself, but without self-nurturing your life threatens to become one monotonous and stressful day after another. You drag yourself out of bed in the morning. You snap at your mate/lover/roommate. You hate your once-fulfilling job or you lack the energy to look for a better one. Sex and sensual enjoyment are things of the past. . . .

Sound like a nightmare? Or does it sound like your life? It doesn't have to be this way!

Taking time off allows you to be more efficient when you return to the task at hand. Relaxation is not a treat, it is necessary for your physical and emotional health. And if you value your time and set limits on what you do for others, others will value your time and treat you with more respect.

If you need more prodding, take a second, look up from this book, and realize that *this is it.* This is life. Your life. Are you doing what you want? Are you getting what you need? Are you loving and caring for yourself? And if not, why not? Remember the venerable axiom: before you can take good care of someone else, you must first take good care of yourself!

You'll Need:

A calendar or date book.

Your journal and pen.

A timer.

When to Do It:

- When reading this book makes you anxious because you can't think of how you are going to fit all these things into your schedule.
- When reading this book makes you sad because, although you would like to, you know you'll never find the time to nurture yourself.
- When you find yourself saying, "It's December? Where did the year go?"
- When the only way you are ever going to take care of yourself is by writing it in a date book.

What to Do:

Time-Is-Life List

Time is the raw material you sculpt into life. Do you believe that? Or do you feel that others dictate how you spend your time?

Get a piece of paper, and make three categories across the top:

LIKE DISLIKE AMBIVALENT ABOUT

Think of a typical week in your life. Under the proper category, list all the activities you did during this week. For example, you might write:

LIKE	DISLIKE	AMBIVALENT ABOUT
Making love	Cleaning the bathtub	Watching TV
Exercise class	Exercise class	Exercise class
Reading a good book	Paying the mortgage	Talking on the phone to mom

Examine the activities you listed under *Dislike*. Go down the list and ask yourself, "Must I do this? And if I must, how can I change this to make it more satisfying or agreeable?" Realize it is impossible to get rid of all the disliked items on your list, but do eliminate or transform as many as you can. Be creative. Brainstorm about how to rid yourself of these activities. Set a timer for ten minutes, and list every idea you can think of. Try to keep your hand moving. Repeat items if you need to. Now take one action to eliminate or change a disliked activity. For example, you could get someone else to physically write the mortgage check; you could move; you could write the check while enjoying a massage or eating lobster in the nude; you could write an entire year of mortgage checks, address and stamp the envelopes, and have your secretary or reliable friend mail them each month. . . . See? Some of the ideas are silly, some worth exploring.

But what about the activities you wrote under *Ambivalent About?* These are probably your time devourers, simply because you are ambivalent about them. You might want to replace some of these with activities you like more. Read on to find out how.

Peak Times

Spend a few days checking in with yourself and determining when you are full of energy and when you're not. Learn to protect and build on these zips of energy. For instance, after you come home from work you may feel drained. This is a good time to do housework, pay bills, return calls, attend to *Dislike* activities that cannot be eliminated. But after dinner, you begin to feel energetic and creative. Nurture that feeling! If the phone rings, let the machine pick it up. Tell your kids you need an hour or two alone. Strive not to let yourself be interrupted. It takes practice and it is not always possible to succeed, but recognize these bursts of energy as valuable cocreators. With them, you can create the life you want and the time to nurture yourself.

How to Rescue Time for Self-Nurturing

See "Creative Selfishness" for help in saying no.

Use an answering machine to screen your calls.

Practice getting off the phone with people who won't shut up. "I'm really glad you called but I can't talk." Try not to make excuses.

Leave the house so you can't hear the phone.

Take the phone off the hook.

Set up phone hours, and tell your friends that is when you will be available.

Choose what you watch on TV. When the program is over, *immediately* turn the machine off.

Give your TV away.

Ride a train, taxi, or carpool to work, and do something instead of driving. I knew one woman who, when it wasn't her turn to drive the forty-five-minute-commute, would cover her eyes with a sleeping mask, put on a Walkman, and meditate through the morning traffic. At first, everyone in the car was miffed, but they became accustomed to her using this time to meet her needs.

Turn off the information overload. You don't have to read every newspaper, magazine, and book out there. You don't have to listen to the news every night.

Let housework go. Try not to use cleaning and straightening as a way to stay busy and avoid nurturing yourself.

Enlist help. If you are married or live with a man, don't let him push the second shift (housework, child care) on to you. You'll only end up resenting him. Divide up the work. In our house I clean, do laundry, and take care of the dog and my garden. My husband cooks, shops, takes out the garbage, and tends his vegetable patch. This should not be considered a unique arrangement.

If you can, give up something in order to have the money to hire a cleaning person once a month.

Don't do housework, or any other tedious work, during your peak times.

Deal with procrastination.

See "The Shadow Side of Comfort" for help.

If you can afford it, buy in bulk. Instead of three greeting cards, buy twenty. Instead of one pair of running shoes or jeans, buy two.

Buy gifts when you see them, then store them.

Consolidate errands. Do everything you can on the phone.

Pick a theme for your holiday gifts, and do much of your shopping in two or three places (books, music, plants, subscriptions, calendars).

Shop by mail.

Ask for help.

Ask for help.

Ask for help.

And finally, regularly query yourself, "Is this how I choose to spend my time?"

Register Your Rapture

Freeing the time and then making sure you use it for self-nurturing are two different challenges. There is a well-known rule that work expands to fill the time available. Once you make the time, you need to be sure you fill it with comforting things. This is especially true when you are trying to replace *Ambivalent* activities with more nurturing ones.

See "Comfort Journal: Investigate What Being Good to Yourself Means" for help coming up with ideas. See also "The Power of Goals: Your Ideal Day" and "A Day Off: Make A Bliss List."

See "A Day Off" for day-long bliss-inspiring ideas.

Dream up a list of pleasurable activities you would love to do. Write these bliss-inspiring ideas in your comfort journal. Think of pleasures that encompass each area of your life: physical, emotional, mental, and spiritual. What is missing in your life? What are you not doing that you wish you were?

Make your list varied in terms of time requirements: activities you can do in a few minutes, an hour, a half day, a day, even two days.

Your list does not have to be made up entirely of solitary pleasures, but some activities you should do alone just to ensure you aren't basing your bliss on someone else's desires. Try to come up with at least twenty pleasures. This will give you variety.

Pleasure Program

Whip out your calendar, and open it to tomorrow. Place your pleasure list next to your calendar. Now on each and every day, schedule two pleasurable activities. Keep an eye out for balance. For example:

MONDAY

Talk to my best friend
Go for a walk

TUESDAY

Meditate for fifteen minutes
Watch a movie with girlfriends

WEDNESDAY

Attend new dance class
Go to library and find books on butterflies

THURSDAY

Draw
Get a massage

FRIDAY

Go to the museum during my lunch hour

Put on music and do spontaneous exercise for twenty minutes
Have a nice dinner with my lover
(Notice you can schedule more than two!)

The goal is to nurture all aspects of yourself and to make a real commitment to it.

And Remember

You are in charge of your life. It may not always seem like it, but you do choose to be too busy or to be bored. I know that may not be a very comforting thought, but it is a liberating one. Try to find the time to care for yourself. Make it a priority. Self-care will enrich your life immeasurably.

RESOURCES:

Self-Nurture: Learning to Care for Yourself as Effectively as You Care for Everyone Else, by Alice Domar, Ph.D. (Penguin, 2001). A lovely, well-researched book!

The Gift of the Year: How to Give Yourself the Most Meaningful, Satisfying, and Pleasurable Year of Your Life, by Mira Kirshenbaum (Plume, 2001). Carve out a year within your current life to follow a dream.

The Family Manager Takes Charge: Getting on the Fast Track to a Happy, Organized Home, by Kathy Peel (Perigee Books, 2003). Delegate—motivate—organize . . . relax!

Websites:

Getting Things Done
http://www.gettingthingsdone.com

The List Organizer
http://www.listorganizer.com

Fly Lady
http://www.flylady.com

EASE INTO COMFORTING YOURSELF

What Is It?

Having a hard time getting into nurturing yourself? Does seriously caring for yourself seem too frivolous? Or perhaps you are overwhelmed, and you suddenly feel you must become the world's best self-nurturer?

My sole intention in writing this book is to make you feel good. Ease into comforting yourself with one or two of the simple suggestions that follow. All that matters is that you feel good about yourself.

You'll Need:

Easy-to-find pleasure items, like a single rose catching the morning light, a hot cup of tea, your fuzzy bathrobe.

When to Do This:

- When you can't get into the idea of nurturing yourself.
- When you are having trouble slowing down or allowing yourself to figure out what is comforting to you.
- When the idea of taking time just for you makes you roar with laughter.

What to Do:

Beginning with Yourself

Serve yourself morning coffee or hot tea in a nice cup. Linger over it in bed or in a patch of sunlight.

Lie in the sun. Let the warmth infuse your soul.

Play a piece of music you love. If your selection is one side of a cassette, tell yourself the world is not going to end if you take twenty minutes to sit still and relax.

For fifteen minutes let yourself be a blob. No movement, no purpose. Exist at the amoeba level. Let your thoughts drift. Think about whatever you want.

Go for a brief early morning walk.

Beginning with yourself | *Connections*
Start nurturing your mind | *Childlike starters*
Natural nurturers | *For your body*

Start Nurturing Your Mind

Affirm yourself. Affirmations are short, upbeat statements written in the present tense. They are used to retrain your unconscious. Try to believe, as you work with your affirmations, that these statements are already true. Examples:

See "Courage Rituals: Affirm Self-Care"; "Nurture Your Body Image"; "Nutritional Music: Personal Comfort Tape"; and "Spirit Succor: Spirit Time" for additional ways to use affirmations for comfort.

I love myself.
I am worth self-care.
I deserve love.
I am a great person.
I approve of myself.

Tack your affirmations inside your medicine cabinet or to your car visor, or carry them inside your purse.

Avoid the news for a few days—TV, newspapers, even "All Things Considered."

Do something you are good at—cooking a meal, playing Trivial Pursuit, gardening. Celebrate your strengths!

Go to the library. Check out books you would normally never let yourself read, like books on astrology or current fiction. Allow yourself to be entertained.

See "Reading like a Child" for more easy ideas.

Natural Nurturers

Watch a sunset. Don't move until it gets completely dark.

Go someplace with a fountain or waterfall. Listen to the water trickling and tinkling.

Eat something natural and raw, like a ripe apple or a luscious strawberry. Concentrate on the taste, the texture, the aliveness of what you are eating. Let its energy course into your body.

Buy yourself a houseplant.

See "Green Things" for help.

Spend a few minutes lying on grass looking at the sky

Connections

Chat with a stranger. Make contact with someone new.

Call someone you care for, and tell them how great you think they are.

Clean out your closet, and give your extra clothes away to a battered women's shelter.

Childlike Starters

Light a sparkler, and carve your name in the air.

Curl up with a blanket, and watch the rain.

Play with a small child.

Listen to a children's choir.

For Your Body

Visit a lake or the ocean, and breathe deeply for five minutes.

Go for a walk in the moonlight.

What have you always wanted to do for yourself, in terms of beauty or body care? Have you always wanted to color your hair? Have a facial? A makeup lesson? Try colored mascara? Do it!

See "Body Delights: Take It All In."

Get a massage.

RESOURCES:

Guided Meditations, Explorations, and Healings, by Stephen Levine (Anchor, 1991). Wide range of guided meditations.

Meditation Secrets for Women: Discovering Your Passion, Pleasure, and Inner Peace, by Camille Maurine and Lorin Roche (HarperSanFrancisco,

2001). An encyclopedia of feminine and body-centered ways to meditate. If you've always thought meditation meant sitting still or following a guru, you need this book.

Creating a Charmed Life: Sensible, Spiritual Secrets Every Busy Woman Should Know, by Victoria Moran (HarperSanFrancisco, 1999). Bite-sized chapters of ways to ease into creating a comfortable life that fits you.

Sacred Pampering Principles: An African-American Woman's Guide to Self-Care and Inner Renewal, by Debrena J. Gandy (Quill, 1998). A comfort book with an emphasis on African-American women.

The Emotional Energy Factor: The Secrets High-Energy People Use to Beat Emotional Fatigue, by Mira Kirshenbaum (Delacorte Press, 2003). A very helpful look at getting rid of what drains your energy.

Busy but Balanced: Practical and Inspirational Ways to Create a Calmer, Closer Family, by Mimi Doe (Griffin, 2001). An elegant, realistic how-to manual.

Office Spa: Stress Relief for the Working Week, by Darrin Zeer with illustrations by Frank Montagna (Chronicle Books, 2002). Simple, effective do-anywhere techniques.

Health Journeys: Total Wellness, by Belleruth Naparstek (Time Warner Audio, 2001). Belleruth is the queen of healing imagery. This is an audio two-pack of meditations and affirmations for dealing with stress and creating wellness. Superb!

Joyful Mind, by Susan Piver (Audio). Two-CD sampler of seven different kinds of meditations, including vipassana, zazen, shamatha, metta, toglen, and yoga.

Websites:

Health Journeys—visit their
Desktop Spa
http://www.healthjourneys.com

Comfort Queen
http://www.comfortqueen.com

Seven Masters
http://www.7masters.com

Positive Press
http://www.positivepress.com

YOUR NURTURING VOICE

What Is It?

Self-nurturing means, above all, making a commitment to self-compassion, to the creation of a loving and positive attitude toward yourself. That does not mean you see yourself as perfect or deny all your faults. Instead, you strive to see the positive, to encourage yourself, and to accept yourself like a loving parent or best friend.

We all have an internal monologue chattering away in our heads. Unfortunately, our critical voice, the voice that is never satisfied, never happy, tends to dominate our nurturing voice, the inner voice of encouragement and compassion.

We need to activate and strengthen this inner nurturing voice and make it available to ourselves at all times. If we don't know how to give ourselves approval, we are left begging for approval from everyone else. Either we can waste a lot of precious time and energy manipulating others to give us the recognition we crave, or we can learn to appreciate and acknowledge ourselves. Developing a self-nurturing voice is a key step in meeting our own needs.

Your nurturing voice is an incredible comfort to carry around with you. She can make the hardest times, the deepest depressions, and the greatest challenges easier. She can help you strive for and accomplish goals you never even dreamed of. And her, actually *your*, strokes of recognition feel wonderful.

You'll Need:

Your journal and a pen.

When to Do This:

- When someone puts you down or makes you doubt yourself.
- When you are so low you can hardly move.
- Any time you need a pat on the back, a dose of warm love, a lift of energy.
- When your critical voice is running your life.

What to Do:

Part 1: Listening to Yourself

Draw a line down the middle of several pieces of paper. On the left side, write down every negative thing you say or think about yourself today. Listen to yourself.

Part 1: listening to yourself	*Resistance to your nurturing voice*
Part 2: responding	*Daily nurturing strokes*

Pay attention to internal statements like, "I screwed the presentation up. That's typical!" or "Jeez, I look ugly today" or "If I get any fatter!" Write down this insidious negative chatter.

Note any compliments you routinely reject. "This dress? Oh, it's as old as the hills" or "No way, I haven't lost weight. I look like a cow."

Watch for self-deprecating or negative statements you make to others about yourself.

Write all of these down.

Part 2: Responding

Put your paper nearby, with a pen. **Relax.** Now, imagine a hand coming to rest on your right hand. The hand feels very familiar and loving. It is a healing hand. This hand belongs to the part of you that accepts you as you are right now, at this very instant.

Feel the accepting warmth of this hand resting comfortingly on yours. Slowly draw this warmth along your arm and throughout your body. You are becoming alive with the acceptance and love this healing hand has given you.

Gently open your eyes, pick up your pen, and begin writing, on the right side of the paper, positive replies to the criticisms you recorded on the left side. Give a voice to the healing energy now inside you. This is your nurturing voice.

Let this new inner voice respond to all the negative criticisms you wrote on the left side of the paper. Step back and let your nurturing voice flow through you. Create a dialogue. Here is an example from my journal.

I look like crap today.

No, you don't. You're just a little tired. Why don't you wear your favorite dress today?

I really blew it at work.

You made a mistake. No one is perfect. You are not accustomed to criticism. Forgive yourself.

Convert all those negatives into supportive positives. This has nothing to do with conceit and everything to do with affirming what is great about you.

Resistance to Your Nurturing Voice

You may feel uncomfortable and not believe your nurturing voice, especially as she gains strength and takes off, offering you support all on her own.

Get a new piece of paper. Write down one particularly virulent negative statement. A negative statement that drones through your mind often is especially good.

Let your nurturing voice respond with a positive. Then let your critic respond. Here's an example from my journal:

I hate my body. I feel fat and bloated and ugly.

I love your body. I love how strong and sleek you are. I love the way you bounce when you walk.

What about my tree trunk thighs?

You can climb mountains and canoe in the wilderness. You can protect yourself. I love how strong you are.

Okay, Pollyanna, what about my wrinkles?

What's wrong with wrinkles? I'm proud of what a strong person you're becoming. I'm proud of all you have learned about life.

Sometimes, I doubt I've learned anything.

Well, don't. You are becoming very wise. And you are funny and sexy.

Really?

Continue until your critic begins to absorb the nurturing voice's affection. Work with your resistance. Use it to your advantage. Your nurturing voice will become stronger and stronger, defeating your critic more resoundingly every time. It takes time, and it can often feel like you're just making it all up, but that's fine. You are on the right track.

See "Courage Rituals: I-Am-Worthwhile Meditation Ritual" for encouragement.

Daily Nurturing Strokes

Incorporate your nurturing voice into your life on a daily basis. Talk with her in the car on your way to and from work. Allow a constant stream of supportive talk to flow in your head. Let her dialogue with your critic when you are feeling stomped on.

Don't be discouraged if you forget to listen to your nurturing voice. It is easier for us to be negative with ourselves. Remember your critical voice has had years of practice. Don't worry; just start giving yourself loving strokes again.

See "Reminding Yourself."

RESOURCES:

Taming Your Gremlin: A Surprisingly Simple Method for Getting Out of Your Own Way, by Rick Carson (Quill, 2003). The classic on talking back to your inner critic.

Embracing Your Inner Critic: Turning Self-Criticism into a Creative Asset, by Hal Stone and Sidra Stone (HarperSanFrancisco, 1993). A primer for including and listening to all of your selves.

There Is Nothing Wrong with You: Going Beyond Self-Hate, by Cheri Huber (Zen Meditation Center, 2001). Available at http://www.thezencenter.org/books.html.

Websites:

A Daily Affirmation
http://www.yourdailyaffirmation.com

CREATIVE SELFISHNESS

What Is It?

Creative selfishness is behavior that allows you to care for yourself without feeling guilty. Creative selfishness is taking the time to live your life with respect for you!

We have all been indoctrinated to be unselfish. To even suggest selfish behavior smacks of heresy. Study a woman who practices unselfishness, and you may see a manipulative martyr who tries to win love and sympathy by practicing "good" behavior. Look at the words: *unselfish* and *selflessness*. No self!

Isn't caring for others an important part of life? Yes! But only if you are caring and doing for others because you honestly feel rewarded by it, not because you're telling yourself this is what you are supposed to do to be a "good woman." Caring for others in order to be "good" means living without self-respect, and over time it is tantamount to self-destruction.

Creative selfishness sends a clear message to everyone in your life: I love you (or value you or respect you), but I am a separate person with needs of my own. By practicing creative selfishness, not only will you gain the time to care for yourself, you will also gain the respect of the significant people in your life.

Creative selfishness, like all self-nurturing activities, will help you amass an overflow of love that will allow you to care for others from your abundance. That is truly being a "good woman"!

You'll Need:

Courage.

When to Do It:

- When the idea of taking time for yourself is so foreign you needed someone to explain the concept to you.
- When the idea of saying no to someone makes you cringe.
- When you have no idea what a personal boundary is.

What to Do:

Eliminate Guilt

Learning to be assertive is invaluable in helping you to escape the trap of taking care of

Eliminate guilt	*Say no*
Be firm	*More help saying the "N" word*
Define your boundaries	*Be patient*

others' needs before your own. *You are the only caretaker of your self-esteem.* This means, if you don't assert yourself, if you don't champion your rights, who is going to?

Acknowledge aloud and often that you are not responsible for everyone's feelings. This does not mean you don't care. To be empathetic is wonderful, but you need not feel guilty, ashamed, or responsible for another person's feelings.

But what if you still feel guilty? Try these suggestions:

Stop taking the blame for things that are not your fault. To accomplish this, before you say "I'm sorry" to someone, check to see if you had any control of what happened. I don't know how many times I have said "I'm sorry" when a friend is sick. My empathy is fine, but I need to be clear that their illness is not my fault.

Take the time to explore your guilt in your journal. Free-associate with the words *guilt*, *responsibility*, and *selfishness*. Reflect a few days later on what you wrote. Have your nurturing voice debate with your guilty voice about what you wrote.

See "Your Nurturing Voice: Resistance to Your Nurturing Voice" for an example of dialogue.

In your journal, try answering the question, "What am I getting out of feeling guilty?"

Acknowledge you feel guilty, but don't let it stop you.

You are not alone. Most women feel guilty when they put their needs first. Get together with a couple of friends and talk about your guilt.

See "A Forgiveness Ritual" and "Women for Comfort: Form a Support Club."

Be Firm

See "Solitude."

You decide to take the weekend off. You plan to spend it in a nearby inn, reading and going for walks. Alone. You have told everyone who needs to know. Thursday night your partner tells you he or she has planned a dinner party for Saturday night.

You: That sounds lovely.

Your Partner: But you know I can't cook. I can't do this alone!

You: I told you three weeks ago what my plans were.

Your Partner: I forgot. Can't you change your plans?

You: No. I need this weekend, and I am sticking to my plan.

See "Comforting Communication" for communication remedies.

No angry accusations or critical reactions. Avoid "I'm sorry" and guilty excuses. Empathy and firm resolve. (Note: This is an ideal example. It can be very difficult to be this clear and firm. It doesn't hurt to try.)

Define Your Boundaries

Consciously set your boundaries. Define your limits to yourself. Write down what you will and will not accept. Does your son's borrowing your car without asking invade your boundaries? Does someone's standing too close to you make you crazy? Your limits exist naturally. You know that your boundaries are being invaded when you feel taken for granted. Not being honest with others about your personal limits will leave you feeling depressed, betrayed, and angry. Begin to gently but clearly tell people in your life what your limits are. Realize you may change your boundaries at any time.

Say No

How often do you say yes when you want to shout no? Do you say yes because you will feel guilty if you don't? Because you are afraid of what They will think? We spend so much of our lives worrying about Them. I wonder if They all live in a room somewhere with a giant telescope that allows Them to see everything we do.

Saying no in an assertive, not aggressive, manner is hard. The person making the request is asking you for something. That person wants you to say yes. Don't look to them for help when making your decision.

Ask yourself, is this a reasonable request? Check your body. Are you breathing shallowly? Are you perspiring? Do you feel trapped, pushed into a corner? No one is going to hate you if you say no when you need to. You are not going to become a selfish meanie who lives alone in a decaying shack with fifty cats. People will respect you!

More Help Saying the "N" Word

Visualize yourself saying no. Practice saying the word aloud, perhaps in front of a mirror. Do this before you talk to someone you know will try to pressure you into saying yes.

Abolish "I'm sorry but . . ." before your no. Forget long-winded excuses. Simple, direct explanation will do. Does the shoe salesman need to know why you can't buy the boots? No. But your best friend does need to know why you can't baby-sit.

Some people will try to make you feel guilty. Dig in your heels. Just keep repeating no. Use your anger at their manipulation to stay firm. You have the right to choose what you will and won't do. Are you doing what you honestly want to do or what you feel others want you to do?

In the next week, say no to four things you would normally agree to. For instance, don't pick up the phone like you usually would during your solitude time. At the same time, say yes to four things you would usually not let yourself have. For example, allow yourself to talk on the phone long-distance to your best friend for as long as you want without feeling guilty. If you would say yes or no anyway, it doesn't count. Try to pay attention to how you feel about these changes.

Be Patient

Don't let your inner critic stomp all over you if you can't immediately say no or find time for yourself. Let your natural interests and zest for life (and maybe the suggestions in this book) provide your motivation for creative selfishness.

RESOURCES:

Daily Meditations for Women Who Do Too Much, by Anne Wilson Schaef (HarperSanFrancisco, 2000). Meditation book about the importance of self-nurturing.

Asserting Yourself—A Practical Guide for Positive Change, by Sharon Bower and Gordon Bower (Addison-Wesley, 1991). More help.

Where to Draw the Line: How to Set Healthy Boundaries Every Day, by Anne Katherine (Simon and Schuster, 2000). By setting boundaries you protect your time and energy for the things that matter most!

The Bitch in the House: Twenty-Six Women Tell the Truth About Sex, Solitude, Work, Motherhood, and Marriage, by Cathi Hanauer (William Morrow, 2002). Candid essays by mothers, lovers, wives, and independent women about the reality of living in the taffy-pull world of household responsibility and work. No solutions, but you will feel less alone.

Flux: Women on Sex, Work, Love, Kids, and Life in a Half-Changed World, by Peggy Orenstein and Alice Van Straalen (Knopf, 2001). Interviews with hundreds of women about how they combine work and family, how they navigate society and personal perceptions of what women should do.

Addiction to Perfection, by Marion Woodman (Inner City Books, 1982). The classic Jungian study of how perfection kills women.

How Much Joy Can You Stand? How to Push Past Your Fears and Create Your Dreams, by Suzanne Falter-Barns (Wellspring/Ballantine, 2000). A practical, hands-on dig into your dreams and inspirations. Visit http://www.howmuchjoy.com for more information.

Confessions of an Organized Homemaker: The Secrets of Uncluttering Your Home and Taking Control of Your Life, by Deniece Schofield (Betterway, 1994). From meal planning to cleaning to clutter management.

The Marriage Sabbatical: The Journey That Brings You Home, by Cheryl Jarvis (Broadway Books, 2002). How to find time for yourself while staying married.

COMFORT RITUALS

What Is It?

The human spirit loves rituals. Rituals connect us to wonder, to self-discovery, to the world of myths and symbols. They offer a metaphoric means to help us take responsibility for our lives. The ritual process brings us renewed balance, empowerment, energy, and comfort. Rituals help us live our lives more consciously. Most importantly, rituals provide a way to connect us to our spirits.

But what is a comfort ritual? A comfort ritual is a ritual that focuses on self-nurturing. It allows you to create a specific, delineated time in which to focus on nursing yourself and your feelings. By setting aside time for nurturing rituals, you are performing sacred self-care, which simply means you're making a connection with your inner self. Using the ancient power of ritual for self-care can turn simple behaviors into life-affirming messages.

The rituals in this book are only suggestions. They are not inherently sacred. Feel free to change and personalize whatever you want. The most effective rituals are always personal. Be guided by what feels right to you.

You'll Need:

A candle.

Books of poetry or inspiration.

Dried sage.

Any fireproof dish that doesn't get hot to the touch.

When to Do It:

- After a long illness.
- After a hideous day at work.
- During a period of transition, like divorce, marriage, moving to a new house.
- When you are often so drained or depressed that you need comfort you can easily slip into.

What to Do:

Going-to-Sleep Ritual

The key to making a daily ritual effective is to make it repetitive. Listen to the same music, light a candle, perform it in the same space. This helps focus your mind and heart.

See "Herbal Help" for relaxing tea and bath recipes and "Bathing Pleasures" for bathing rituals.

See "Reminding Yourself" for uplifting titles.

Select something special to wear. Consider partaking of some herbal tea or enjoying a relaxing bath.

Light a candle or two by your bed. Turn off the other lights. Stretch across your bed, taking your time, exaggerating your movements. Feel the cool sheets against your body. Moving slowly, open a book of poetry (or an uplifting or thought-provoking book), and slowly read a page. Allow the wisdom and beauty of what you are reading to enter your mind. Put the book aside. Take a minute to concentrate on the candle flame. Blow out the candle, and curl into peaceful sleep.

Morning Ritual

Spend ten minutes holding, talking, and just existing with the person you share your life with. Make this a priority in your daily life, no matter how busy.

You can do this if you're alone. Take a few moments to imagine your day going beautifully. Snuggle down in your warm sheets, and hug yourself. Stretch like a cat. Repeat a few times to yourself, "This is going to be a great day."

See "Animal Antidotes."

Letter to Yourself

Every second day for a week or so, write a letter to yourself. Write about the things you are proud of, your goals, your worries, your frustrations. Address these letters to yourself, and mail them.

When they return to you, read them in a quiet place. Pretend you have never seen them before. Allow your letters to be the voice of your inner self, messages to be decoded.

Explore Your Current Rituals

Examine the rituals that you practice in your life, like reading the morning newspaper, watching the news at night, eating Sunday dinner. Strive to be aware if stale, formalized rituals are cutting you off from life. Sit down and give a few minutes of thought to how you could revitalize those rituals. Try brainstorming ideas in your comfort journal.

An example of a stale ritual: You share dinner with your partner every night. During dinner, you watch TV. You realize this ritual leaves you feeling dull and disconnected. One way to change this is to reinvent dinner once or twice a week. Try candlelight and nice dishes. Tell each other five things that happened that day. A few days later, try eating in the nude and feeding each other with your hands. You could experiment with blessing the meal and talking about spiritual concerns while eating simple food.

Blessing Ritual

You can use this ritual for dedicating your personal sanctuary or a new home.

Lay some sage in a fireproof dish, with matches nearby. Sage is used by Native Americans as a purifying herb.

Spend a few minutes composing a blessing. Create a blessing that speaks from your heart. My example:

I invoke the ancient power of this land where our house stands.

This primordial power protects our house at all times.

Our house will be safe from crime, fire, flood, and earthquake.

From plumbing problems and bugs.

My garden will flourish, held sacred by this land.

Our house will be a sanctuary for all who enter, a home filled with love and comfort.

Blessed be.

When you are ready, light your sage. Walk through the area you are blessing, fanning the smoke while repeating, singing, or chanting your blessing.

Spend a few minutes visualizing your blessing coming true. Fill your mind with happy scenes and your heart with feelings of safety and well-being.

Rebirthing Ritual

This is based on Barbara Walker's rebirthing ritual from her book *Women's Rituals*.

See "Creating a Comfort Network" and "Spirit Succor: Spiritual Nurturing with Others."

This ritual can be done alone or with several close friends. It is an especially powerful ritual to do after being sick, when a divorce is final, or before a marriage.

Construct a spiral using cushions and pillows on the floor. Imagine the inside of a seashell. The inner chamber or "womb" should be almost entirely enclosed. Make a warm, soft bed with pillows and quilts.

Music helps this ritual. Play something that has a slow, steady beat. If you are doing this with friends, consider having one of them beat time on a drum.

Stand at the opening of the spiral. Close your eyes and immerse yourself in a feeling of safety. Let your worries fly away. You are entering sacred space.

Walk slowly into the spiral. Pause often to feel yourself breathing and to imagine your problems peeling away from you, being left behind.

When you reach the inner chamber, curl up in the fetal position. Place your hand on your heart and feel your heartbeat. Exist at the most simple and contented level you can. Stay here as long as you like.

When you are ready to rebirth, let your primal mind take over. Pretend you are actually being born. Or walk calmly out, while you imagine yourself emerging as a new being, ready for new challenges. Trust this moment. Let yourself go.

After you are "born," consider taking a warm bath and reflecting on what you have experienced. Or hug your friends.

You can repeat this ritual on a small scale by building just the "womb" in the middle of your bed. Prepare by breathing slowly, then curl up inside your "womb." Come out when you feel ready, and repeat something like:

I am reborn and refreshed

Ready for a new life.

Parent Yourself

Develop a parenting ritual for the little girl inside you. Search back in your childhood, and try to remember how your loved ones comforted you. Perhaps your mother laid your clothes out every night before school or your aunt packed comforting food to eat at lunch before the big Christmas pageant. Recreate a few of these rituals for the adult you.

Good-Bye Book

Saying good-bye to people, whether for a long time or for just a few weeks, can be difficult.

Create a good-bye ritual with a good-bye book. Similar to your comfort journal, your good-bye book can include pictures of the people leaving, stories about shared experiences, and mementos.

Sit down with the person who is leaving. Leaf though the book together, sharing memories. Agree on a ritual for staying in touch, for instance, Sunday night phone calls or a postcard a week. Write this keeping-in-touch ritual in your good-bye book.

If you don't feel comfortable sharing the good-bye book with the person who is leaving, do it alone soon after they leave. Write your feelings in your good-bye book. If you are afraid of being overwhelmed by your feelings, provide a structure for the ritual with a timer. When it goes off, put the book away and, with it, your pain.

RESOURCES:

The Art of Ritual, by Renee Beck and Sydney Barbara Metrick (Celestial Arts, 1991). How to create your own rituals.

The Book of New Family Traditions: How to Create Great Rituals for Holidays and Everydays, by Meg Cox (Running Press, 2003). A fantastic manual that is not just for families.

Joy of Ritual: Spiritual Recipes to Celebrate Milestones, Ease Transitions, and Make Every Day Sacred, by Barbara Biziou (Golden Books Adult Publishing, 1999). More very helpful ideas—more New Age than Cox's book.

Calling the Circle: The First and Future Culture, by Christina Baldwin (Bantam, 1998). The most comprehensive book about using circle to create change and healing.

Sacred Circles: A Guide to Creating Your Own Women's Spirituality Group, by Robin Carnes (HarperSanFrancisco, 1998). More specific to women's groups.

Circle of Stones: Woman's Journey to Herself, by Judith Duerk (Innisfree Press, 1990). The poetic mythic journey into the core issues of our lives.

Soul Sisters: The Five Sacred Qualities of a Woman's Soul, by Pythia Peay (Jeremy Tarcher, 2002). A workbook designed to help you develop your spiritual life by learning from the heroines from a vast array of spiritual traditions.

The Joyful Family: Meaningful Activities and Heartfelt Celebrations for Connecting with the Ones You Love, by Judy Ford (Conari, 2002). Well organized with a focus on creating bridges and resolving conflicts, growing closer as a family, however you define family.

A PERSONAL SANCTUARY

What Is It?

We all need a space we can call our own. A private territory where we can cherish ourselves without fear of being censored. A place where we can read books, meditate, and work in our journals. A wall to hang nurturing art and affirmations on. A view, a fireplace, soft colors, comfortable furniture. . . .

Sounds heavenly, but the reality is often small children, crowded apartments, and not enough money. How can we create a space that satisfies our need for privacy?

You'll Need:

Your journal and your basket of art supplies.

Home magazines and design books would be helpful.

Whatever else you need will depend upon what your budget allows and what your fantasies require.

When to Do It:

- When you feel you have no space to call your own.
- When you feel restricted from experimenting with self-nurturing activities, for example, meditating, because you don't have the space to practice in.
- When you crave privacy.

What to Do:

Fantasy Sanctuary

Put physical and monetary considerations aside for a moment. Open your journal and arrange your supplies nearby. This has nothing to do with your artistic ability.

Relax. Imagine that you have been given the resources to plan and build the personal space of your dreams. You can create this space anywhere you choose. It can be a room added onto your house, a pagoda in a rain forest, an entire house devoted to nurturing you.

Visualize yourself walking around your place, looking at each detail. Where are you? What is the weather like? What kind of furniture is there? What does it smell like? What would you do here?

Take as long as you like to imagine your fantasy sanctuary. Then open your eyes and draw your interpretation of what you just visualized. Include color, atmosphere, all the details that spark your imagination. Or describe your fantasy in writing.

Reality and Fantasy Meet

Examine your fantasy to determine what you must have. Maybe your dream sanctuary includes a view of a waterfall and a forest, yet you live in Manhattan. Take another look. Maybe your fantasy also includes walls painted a gentle violet, Beethoven playing softly, and two goldfish.

Rank your fantasy in order of importance. What can't you live without? What would you spend money on first?

Find the Space

This is the challenging part. Take a careful look at your home. Where could you create your inner sanctum? If you have a large house with lots of extra rooms, space is probably not a problem for you. But for a lot of women, space is a consideration. Get creative. Is there a room that can do double duty, like a den, home office, guest room, breakfast nook, alcove, service porch, window seat, a corner of a dining room or bedroom, even a large closet?

The key to making a personal space a true sanctuary is to define it in such a way that when you are in it, you are automatically reminded that this time is for you, that you have created an intimate place in which to focus your awareness on self-care.

Practical Design Ideas—Screens

Use decorative or acoustic screens to partition a corner of a room. Making screens is not difficult, and you can buy many different kinds. Try anything from a salvaged elevator grill to an office divider.

See "Heal Your Habitat: Keep It Simple" for how to make a screen.

Hang blinds from the ceiling. Venetian, cane, paper, or roller blinds are inexpensive and can provide interesting textures or a solid wall of color.

Build a wall of shelves, creating a hidden nook. Or press existing free-standing shelves into service. You may want to paint the backs of the shelves or cover them with fabric.

A wall of plants can provide privacy and the feeling of being in a jungle or forest. Be sure to protect your floors and to provide enough light. Dead plants are not comforting.

Hang large, framed posters or mirrors from the ceiling, creating a wall to sequester yourself behind.

Define an Area

Choose a soft rug or a grass mat to distinguish your sanctuary. This is great if your alone time includes meditation or yoga.

Construction

If you are handy at building things, try constructing a cabinet that, when opened, expands into a miniature room, the doors accordion screens that fold out for privacy. Include bookshelves, a drop-leaf desk, and a reading light.

Instant Privacy

A Walkman gives you a world unto yourself. You can use one when you need privacy at home, on a plane, or even at work. Make a comfort tape.

See "Nutritional Music: Personal Comfort Tape."

Outside Your House

What about the garden, your garage, your car? A library can be a good place, especially a corner carrel. One idea is to have a sanctuary both inside your home and outside. The key is to pick a place that you can easily and consistently visit.

A Comfort Box

See "Comfort Journal: A Collage of Comforting Images" for how-to and "A Personal Sanctuary: A Comfort Kit" for a variation.

For a variation on, or in addition to, your personal sanctuary, you could collect comfort things in a special box. Children's books, a stuffed animal, your art supplies: whatever you use to make yourself feel good. Then, when you're ready to nurture yourself, your supplies are easily available to inspire you. You could consider decorating your box with a comfort collage.

RESOURCES:

A Room of One's Own, by Virginia Woolf (Harcourt Brace Jovanovich, 1929). An essay about the importance of women having rooms of their own (and fixed incomes!) to create, think, and be in.

Altars Made Easy: A Complete Guide to Creating Your Own Sacred Space, by Peg Streep (HarperSanFrancisco, 1997). A good basic book to start with.

A Book of Women's Altars: How to Create Sacred Spaces for Art, Worship, Solace, Celebration, by Nancy Brady Cunningham and Denise Geddes (Red Wheel/Weiser, 2002). "An altar helps you to quickly focus on the spirituality inherent in common things."

Move Your Stuff, Change Your Life: How to Use Feng Shui to Get Love, Money, Respect and Happiness, by Karen Rauch Carter (Fireside, 2000). Some cheesy humor, but I like this book because much of feng shui seems way too serious for me.

Holy Personal: Looking for Small Private Places of Worship, by Laura Chester with Donna De Mari (Indiana University Press, 2000). Inspiration for your private space.

CREATING A COMFORT NETWORK

What Is It?

When I first conceived this book, I focused on designing exercises you could do alone. One day, I suddenly realized that taking care of yourself does not mean doing it all alone. We hunger to be heard and to be valued. We must share aspects of our lives with other people.

Realizing we are not alone on the planet, that we are part of the tangle of humanity, helps put our problems and challenges into perspective.

You cannot do it all alone. And why try? There is real magic in each person you know, and that magic is multiplied by the people your people know (and so on). All that magic is just waiting to be tapped, to enliven your life and help you fulfill your dreams.

You'll Need:

Your journal and drawing supplies.

Your address book.

Loving, honest, nurturing people. (They do exist!)

When to Do It:

- When you feel you have lots of friends but are unsure whom to call when you need help or a pep talk.
- When you find yourself more down or uptight after speaking to someone you had hoped would make you feel better.
- When you feel you need a more varied support system.
- When you are lonely.

What to Do:

Who Supports You?

The questions below will help you identify the strengths and weaknesses in your present comfort network.

Who supports you?
Who is comforting, and who is not?
Pick people you trust
Listen to your body
No one listens
Strengthen your comfort network
Ask
Address book
Professional support
Buddy system

Questions:
Name three people you get in touch with when you are blue.

Do these people usually make you feel better?

Who energizes you?

Who do you like to play with?

Name two people you would contact in a crisis. Do you feel you could count on these people to be there for you no matter what, and that they would not make you feel guilty or needy? Would they bring you food if you were ill? Would you feel comfortable giving them your house key?

At work, whom do you seek out when you need honest feedback? Do they help you? Can you trust them?

Whom would you like to discover new things with? Who would you enjoy traveling with?

Is there someone you can discuss spiritual ideas and concerns with?

For now, simply contemplate your answers.

Who Is Comforting, and Who Is Not?

The basic building block of choosing people to comfort you is to talk to the right people at the right time. The people in your life are good for different things at different times. You may have a close friend who can't give you comfort when you are depressed. She may be perfect to celebrate with but not right to grieve with. Recognize this.

Pick People You Trust

Think for a minute about people you trust. Define trust for yourself. Does it mean someone who won't steal from you? Or someone who won't divulge your secrets, even to her husband or lover? Does it mean different things for the different people in your life? Open your comfort journal, and write about trust for fifteen minutes. Try to keep your hand moving, even if you have to repeat words or write nonsense. This technique helps you reach deeper, less logical, knowledge about yourself.

Listen to Your Body

Do you feel fatigued after spending time with a friend? Do you find yourself clenching your jaw during phone conversations, or is your stomach full of flutters? Do you breathe shallowly around certain people?

Your body provides clues to hidden conflicts. Become sensitized to your body's reactions to people. Use that information to help you contact the right person for the right situation. Stay away from people who make you feel trapped, crazy, or invisible. Don't ask people to empathize with you who don't know how. They may be good for other things, but they are not good for nurturing.

See "Creative Selfishness: Define Your Boundaries" and "Creative Selfishness: Say No."

No One Listens

If you feel abandoned and rejected by the people in your life, ask yourself if you are expecting others to take on your feelings, to cure you. Don't blame yourself, just check in to see what your expectations are.

Strengthen Your Comfort Network

Use the questions you answered to identify the weakness in your network. Do you find you have no one to play squash with? Or to dance in the rain or be a kid with? Or no one to talk to about being pregnant? You can find people everywhere to make your life richer: continuing education, the gym, neighborhood watch, Thursday night bingo. . . . Decide to view each and every situation tomorrow as an opportunity to make a friend or resource contact. Be creative and open. Be persistent when necessary. Realize making friends takes time. Keep trying.

Start by picking three people with whom you would like to strengthen your relationship. Write down one step you would be willing to take toward this improvement. Examples could be an invitation to take a walk together, dropping by half a pot of soup you made, sharing business advice. Take one of these steps now.

See "Women for Comfort" and "Nurture Others" for more ideas.

Creating a Comfort Network

See "Courage Rituals."

Ask

Don't be afraid to ask for help or friendship. This may be the hardest part because we fear rejection all the way down to our toes. It may seem too needy to want to be someone's friend. Go ahead, take the risk.

Address Book

When you meet someone you like or who might be a good resource write down her or his address and phone number. Keep in touch with brief postcards that tell her or him how you're doing. Keep your network alive.

Professional Support

Do you feel comfortable with your doctor, attorney, grocer, and accountant? Try new ones until you find professional people you can trust. Don't pay your money for services that leave you feeling unsure, creepy, or insecure.

Shop at friendly places where you feel safe. Don't patronize a store that leaves you feeling bad, just because it is convenient or trendy.

Connect with your neighbors. Having close by someone you can count on for small emergencies is invaluable.

Buddy System

See "Comforting Communication: Be Direct."

A key to having a good support system is being a good supporter to others. Tell people their work is good or their house is cozy. Tell new friends, "I like you. I want to spend more time with you." Offer to help people who might need your expertise. Don't devalue yourself by thinking no one needs you.

Don't always unload on the same friend. If you have been depressed or grieving for a long period of time, respect the other person's right to get tired and burned out. They can love you and still not be able to offer you anything more right now. No one is supportive or comforting all the time. Respect that other people have bad days or are busy or overloaded with their own problems.

RESOURCES:

Girlfriends' Getaway: A Complete Guide to the Weekend Adventure That Turns Friends into Sisters, by Kathleen Laing and Elizabeth Butterfield (Waterbrook Press, 2002). A lighthearted road guide.

Between Friends: Craft Projects to Share, by Charlotte Lyons and Steven Randazzo (Simon and Schuster, 2002). Create side by side with a friend.

Friendshifts: The Power of Friendship and How It Shapes Our Lives, by Jan Yager (Hannacroix Creek Books, 1999). Solid advice for strengthening connections.

Best Friends: The Pleasures and Perils of Girls' and Women's Friendships, by T. E. Apter and Ruthellen Josselson (Three Rivers Press, 1999). An in-depth study of the challenges and rewards of female friendship.

Heart Deepening: Women's Friendships at Midlife, by Patricia G. Shapiro (Berkeley Publishing Group, 2001). A psychologist interviews fifty women, from ages forty-five to sixty, and blends their stories with research, expert commentary, and her own personal experiences.

Come Rain or Come Shine: Friendships Between Women, by Linda Bucklin (Adams Media, 1999). Hundreds of stories about the importance of maintaining friendships.

I Am a Woman Finding My Voice: Celebrating the Extraordinary Blessings of Being a Woman, by Janet Quinn (Quill, 1999). A powerful book for contemplation.

Websites:

Comfort Queen—help forming your own women's group
http://www.comfortqueen.com

Self-Nurture
http://www.selfnurture.com

Sister I
http://www.sisteri.com

COURAGE RITUALS

What Is It?

What do comfort and courage have to do with each other? Plenty! It may seem like doing good things for yourself should be easy and fun, but for many, many reasons, it often is not. It takes courage, effort, and resolve to care for yourself.

It takes courage to make nurturing yourself a priority. It takes fortitude to meet your own needs. It takes boldness to listen to and trust your intuition. It takes bravery to overcome comfortable but stultifying life patterns. It takes spirit to experience pleasure. It takes heart to come into closer contact with yourself. And finally, it takes strength to live your life in the best possible way, even when there is no one to see but yourself.

Deserving time to care for yourself is not something you earn. You were born deserving self-care. Taking care of yourself is not a reward for getting ten thousand things done today. It is a function of the fact you are alive and deserve nurturing every day. Caring for yourself is not just for thin, successful, rich women. It is for each and every one of us!

You'll Need:

Time, patience, and gentle persistence.

A pen and several sheets of paper.

A small group of friends (optional).

When to Do It:

- When you think other women are better at caring for themselves than you.
- When you are afraid to take care of yourself or you think taking the time to do so equals wasting time.
- When you have set a goal and need an extra dose of courage to help you achieve it.

What to Do:

Name and Recognize

The next time you are afraid to care for yourself, admit it. Aloud. Also, try admitting your fear to someone you trust. Naming and recognizing your fear are crucial steps in taking self-care seriously.

Name and recognize | *Affirm self-care*
I-am-worthwhile meditation ritual | *Courage ritual with friends*

As part of naming your fears and blocks, create a deprivation list. List all the self-nurturing activities you deprive yourself of, and write down all the reasons you do so. Try to be honest. For example, I have to cajole myself into buying and applying body lotion. I have to remind myself I deserve the self-care required in putting on lotion! The reason I do this is because I'm not comfortable with my body. What do you deny yourself? No one will read this list. Write whatever you want.

I-Am-Worthwhile Meditation Ritual

To develop courage is to develop a steadfast belief in the worth of your own life. From this belief, many wonderful things can grow, ranging from the capacity to say no without feeling guilty to the strength to explore a new career.

Pick a time in which you can be alone every day for a week. The key to making a ritual effective is to make it repetitive. Listen to the same music, light a candle, burn incense, or practice it in the same space. This helps focus your mind and heart. Of course, you can enjoy this meditation any time, without making it part of a ritual.

See "A Personal Sanctuary."

You might want to use lotion or massage oil with this meditation.

Close your eyes and **relax.** Focus on your breathing. Realize that each breath you take is irreplaceable, a one-time-only event. Breathe in and out a few times, and let this fact sink in. Now, hold your hands. With your eyes still closed, caress and explore your hands. Absorb the fact that this is the only pair of hands like these in the universe. Nowhere else does this pair of hands exist. Let your hands touch your opposite wrists and forearms. Stroke your skin and muscle. Allow your hands to travel up to your biceps and shoulders. Breathing deeply, hug yourself. Focus on your breath again. Like your breath, each moment of your life is unique and precious. Say to yourself or aloud, "I grant myself the right to exist and flourish. I am worthwhile."

When you are ready, take one more deep, deep breath, sending your conviction of self-worth throughout your body, and open your eyes.

See "Your Nurturing Voice" for help loving yourself.

Affirm Self-Care

See "Ease into Comforting Yourself" for an explanation of affirmations and "Soothing Sounds: Chanting."

Convince your mind you deserve time for self-nurturing. Make a daily ritual out of working with affirmations. Here are some suggestions:

I am a wonderful person and deserve time off.

I now have the courage to live life my way.

I deserve to nurture myself.

Make up your own. Chant an affirmation while driving home from work. Sing a few in the shower. Listen to the voices that are telling you it is not okay to care for yourself, and devise affirmations to shut them up!

Courage Ritual with Friends

See "Creating a Comfort Network" and "Women for Comfort: Form a Support Club."

Choose carefully the people you share your fears with! They should be women with whom you can be intimate, who will respectfully listen and openly share.

Set aside an evening with one or more friends near the full moon. The full moon has been a time of power for women for thousands of years. It is natural and good to connect with that power.

Choose a private location where you can either build a fire or safely light a candle large enough to burn paper over.

Have each woman bring a musical instrument. A small drum, wind chimes, or a children's tambourine are possibilities. You will also need several pieces of paper and a pen for each woman.

Form a circle around the fire.

Hold hands. Close your eyes. Lead your friends in a few moments of breathing. Mention that everything that happens during the course of tonight must be held in confidence.

Now go around the group and let each person talk about a remarkable woman she has admired. Let these women's stories and strengths enter your group.

Pick up your instruments and drum out a beat together. If you relax and trust that the song will unfold and feel empowering, it will. Let the song carry on until it dies out naturally.

See "Soothing Sounds" for help.

Pass out the paper and pens. Ask each woman to write down the fears that are blocking her pursuit of self-care.

Take turns going around the circle, allowing each woman to talk about what she has written. It is a good idea not to interrupt.

After each woman is finished talking, she burns her paper. Together, the group recites a blessing:

We accept that you have fears.

You are not your fears.

You are now cleansed and renewed.

Go forward with courage at your side.

Exchange kisses and hugs around the circle. It feels great to share food and drink now or to go for a brisk walk together.

You can easily do this ritual alone, but don't skimp. Make a circle with flowers or stones, silently reflect or write about a woman you've admired, chant or drum along with a tape, and don't forget to hug yourself afterward.

RESOURCES:

The Courage to Be Yourself: A Woman's Guide to Growing Beyond Emotional Dependence, revised edition (Conari Press, 1991), and *The Woman's Book of Courage* (Conari Press, 1991), both by Sue Patton Thoele. How to get the courage to improve your life.

The Return of Courage, by Jean-Louis Servan-Schreiber (Addison-Wesley, 1987). A philosophical examination of the need for everyday courage.

Elegant Choices, Healing Choices, by Marsha Sinetar (Paulist Press, 1989). Good when you need help making life choices.

Wise Women: A Celebration of Their Insights, Courage, and Beauty, by Joyce Tenneson (Bulfinch Press, 2002). Eighty portraits of women ages sixty-five to one hundred.

Courage: The Joy of Living Dangerously, by Osho (Griffin, 1999). I find his ideas startlingly useful.

Women of Courage: Inspiring Stories from the Women Who Lived Them, by Katherine Martin (New World Library, 1999). Stories in which women we admire describe life-altering moments in which they had to find strength and courage.

The Power of Positive Choices: Adding and Subtracting Your Way to a Great Life, by Gail McMeekin (Conari Press, 2001). An amazingly powerful book to help you hone in on the right choices. Highly useful!

The Courage to Heal: A Guide for Women Survivors of Child Sexual Abuse, by Ellen Bass and Laura Davis (Perennial, 1994). I learned much about self-nurturing from this classic.

Starting Out in the Afternoon, by Jill Frayne (Random House, 2003). A memoir of traveling to the Yukon by car, foot, and kayak from southern Ontario.

Looking for Lovedu: A Woman's Journey Across Africa, by Ann Jones (Vintage, 2002). From Tangier to the tip of South Africa in search of the last Queen of Lovedu.

Music:

Scarlet's Walk by Tori Amos, *Music for Energy and Motivation* by Steven Mark Kohn, *Ain't Nuthin' but a She Thing* by various artists (Salt-N-Pepa, Annie Lennox, Melissa Etheridge, Patti Smith, and Queen Latifah, *Cosmic Thing* by The B-52's, *The Best of the Gipsy Kings* by Gipsy Kings, *Born to Run* by Bruce Springsteen

Websites:

Self-Growth
http://www.selfgrowth.com

Healthy Place
http://www.healthyplace.com

MONEY, MONEY, MONEY

What Is It?

Money makes most of us crazy. It has taken on a powerful life of its own instead of remaining a simple medium of exchange. We have given this neutral commodity too much power, and it is running our lives.

But money is only a state of mind. As "cosmic" as it sounds, our attitude about money is more important than any other single factor. I will even risk stating that our personal attitudes about money are more important than the sexist economy that shackles us. Women are still paid much less than men for the same work. Girls are still brought up to think they cannot understand math. Millions of fathers never pay child support. These are very real issues, and we cannot think them away. But how we think and feel does determine how these concerns affect us. To instigate change, we must start with our state of mind about money. From change comes the power and determination to adjust the larger issues.

You'll Need:

A mirror.

A purse-sized spiral notebook.

When to Do It:

- When you feel uncomfortable spending money on yourself.
- If you have no idea how much your partner earns, what would happen if he or she died, or what kind of savings your family has.
- When you feel depressed about money.
- When you have no idea where your money is spent.

What to Do:

Gratitude Riches

Be grateful for what you do have. This may sound like a stern parental commendation. It isn't. Begin to free yourself from money's

---

Gratitude riches
Self-esteem balance
Mirror your worth
Money journal
Inherit from your intuition
The exchange rate
Historical holdings
Barter leverage

tyrannical grip by taking inventory of all that is good in your life now. Don't concentrate on what is lacking. Don't limit yourself to material things or bank balances. Be grateful for everything in your life: your best friend, Yosemite National Park, your toes. Practice this whenever you hear yourself thinking or saying negative things about money.

Self-Esteem Balance

Our self-esteem is often intimately wrapped up with our bank accounts and salaries. Work to change that. Money is not you, and you are not money! Hold some cash in your hand. Try to see it simply as a medium of exchange. When you get your paycheck, look at it and say, "I earned this money and that's great, but this money is not me."

Mirror Your Worth

Realize that feeling guilty about spending money on yourself reflects a lack of faith and self-value. If you feel uncomfortable or guilty every time you spend money on nurturing yourself, what are you proclaiming? That you aren't worth it. That you don't believe you can earn money and take care of yourself. (If you have a problem with overspending or have a lot of debts, try keeping a journal of your spending habits and focus on the worth of each item.) Spending money on yourself can be a powerful act of love, sending out a message that you believe in your needs, your tastes. Convince yourself that you deserve the things you want and need.

Put a mirror nearby. **Relax.**

Open your eyes and look at yourself in the mirror. Tell yourself aloud, "I deserve (fill in your dream or goal)." For example, "I deserve to be rich beyond my wildest dreams." Or, "I deserve a trip to Tibet." Or, "I deserve money for books to nurture my growth."

You may feel ridiculous. Keep going. Keep looking into your own eyes in the mirror. Keep repeating that you do deserve what you want.

Money Journal

Creating priorities is essential to find the money you need for self-care. Finding the money to nurture yourself means you first must choose to do so. If you spend the rest of your life saying, "after I get a raise" or "after I get the settlement" or "after I sell a book, then I'll do something good for myself," you are never going to do anything.

To decide what your priorities are, create a money journal. Use your small spiral notebook. Create these categories:

AMOUNT SPENT	ON WHAT	FEELINGS
$ .50	candy bar	felt fat afterward
$ 7.00	lunch	boring and rushed
$15.54	books	love them

Keep track for one month of every penny you spend, including regular monthly expenditures like rent or car insurance. Even if you record an expense in your checkbook, jot it in the notebook too. If you quit halfway through a month, just start again the following month. No guilt!

After you have completed a full month, study the patterns. Use your findings to help you choose what to spend your money on in the future. For example, if you find you don't enjoy spending money on lunch during the week, pack your lunch and use the money you save to buy books. By paying attention to how you feel about what you spend, you can rearrange your resources to better suit your real needs.

Inherit from Your Intuition

Next time, before you buy something you want, ask yourself:

Do I really need this?

Why am I buying this?

These are magic questions. They trigger your intuition. They work especially well when you are in doubt or feel conflict about a purchase. Give yourself time to find and hear your inner voice of wisdom.

See "Checking Your Basic Needs: A Good Question"; "The Shadow Side of Comfort: Mindful Comfort"; and "Simplify: Three Good Questions" for additional help activating your inner voice.

The Exchange Rate

Become aware of what you are exchanging for your money. Go out on a shopping expedition for something small that you truly want, like a book or bottle of wine. Take your time selecting your purchase. As you are paying for it, visualize your money being converted into what you are buying.

Practice becoming aware of the exchange that takes place each time you buy something. Take a minute to discover if you are relishing what you are buying. The more you enjoy the exchange, the more you are getting for your money.

Historical Holdings

See "Women for Comfort."

Take political action toward economic equality for women. Protect your economic interests. Do not let your mate keep monetary secrets from you. No matter how much you love and trust the person you are with now, realize relationships can change, and act accordingly. *Make sure you can survive without your partner.*

Pick up books about money and read them for ten minutes a day. Think of your financial life as needing the same kind of creative effort you give the rest of your life.

Consider starting a consciousness-raising group with other women. Discuss money, earnings, and the social problems of today.

Barter Leverage

Money is neutral. You give it a value. Consider bartering for things you want. This may help you get a new perspective on cash. It is a great way to form new relationships. It can also help during a cash flow problem.

See "Nurture Others."

If you think you have no services to barter, think again. Everyone has services to offer for barter. What about your particular talents, like photography or calligraphy? Could you critique poetry? Do you own a special piece of equipment that others might like to use? Are you good at carpentry, plumbing, quilting, caring for horses?

Money Order: The Money Management Guide for Women, by Gail Shapiro (Simon and Schuster, 2001). A comprehensive guide to getting a handle on your money.

The Soul of Money: Transforming Your Relationship with Money and Life, by Lynne Twist (Norton, 2003). Lynne Twist is a global activist and fund-raiser who has raised more than $150 million for charitable causes. She demonstrates how we can replace feelings of scarcity, guilt, and burden with experiences of sufficiency, freedom, and purpose.

Money and the Meaning of Life, by Jacob Needleman (Currency, 1994). An exploration of how we can use money as a tool for breaking out of the prison of more, more, more.

Seven Stages of Money Maturity: Understanding the Spirit and Value of Money in Your Life, by George Kinder (Dell, 2000). The only book I have found that combines perennial spiritual wisdom with modern fiscal how-to.

The Mindful Money Guide: Creating Harmony Between Your Values and Your Finances, by Marshall Glickman (Ballantine Books, 1999). Glickman takes the guesswork and guilt out of spending your money in a way that reflects your values.

The Energy of Money: A Spiritual Guide to Financial and Personal Fulfillment, by Maria Nemeth, Ph.D. (Ballantine Books, 2000). An excellent blend of metaphysical and psychology of money. Not too New Agey.

COMFORTING COMMUNICATION

What Is It?

You have people in your life whom you love and respect, a beautiful web of comfort and support (parents, lovers, roommates, best friends, coworkers, relatives). But it is not always clear how to get nurturing from these people. When you crave contact, you need to know how to ask for it and also how to open up and receive it.

You'll Need:

Significant people in your life to whom you can turn or would like to turn for nurturing.

When to Do It:

- When you are lonely, even though you have a partner or lots of friends and family.
- When you feel no one listens to you.
- When you feel uncomfortable asking someone for a favor or to listen to you.

What to Do:

Allow Yourself to Be Needy

A fundamental element of asking for comfort is allowing yourself to ask, allowing yourself to be nurtured by someone else. It can be difficult to ask for a hug or for someone to listen compassionately. The wonderful thing is, when you take the risk to ask someone directly for what you need, you are already nurturing yourself by simply voicing your need.

Go to your window, open it, and shout, "I need support. I deserve wonderful people who love me and listen to me. This in no way diminishes my ability to survive or thrive as a woman!" (Okay, you don't have to shout. . . .)

Be Direct

Make a list of five people to call when life is rotten. Next time you feel awry, call Barbra,

Allow yourself to be needy
Be direct

Did you hear me?

the first name on your list. She's not home. You don't panic, you have your list. You try Eric. He's home. You alert him that you are in pain and need attention by saying:

I need to talk. Do you have the time to listen?

or

I've had an awful day. Can I talk to you about it right now?

or

I feel bad, and I'm not sure what's wrong. Can we talk?

or

I need some comfort. Do you have some to spare?

By stating clearly that you need an ear, you are not setting yourself up for disappointment by hoping your friend will guess your life is wretched today. By asking if the other person has the time to help, you are respecting that person's privacy and energy.

Did You Hear Me?

In close relationships, what we want more than anything (most of the time) is to know the person we love is listening to us. Try this simple exercise:

Set aside time with your lover/partner/anyone you care about. Make sure you won't be interrupted.

Decide who gets to talk first. For fifteen minutes to a half hour, without any interruptions, the first person talks. And the other person listens, *without speaking*. Avoid making this time a tirade against the other person. Avoid attacking or criticizing, and instead focus on sharing your life and soak in the attention of being listened to.

At the end of your time, your partner *makes no comment*. Instead, he or she repeats the process. It is your turn to listen and, by listening, to nurture.

At the end of the session, you may make a date, a few days later, to discuss any problems or questions that came up. Do not respond now. This gives you both time to reflect on what has been said.

RESOURCES

Getting the Love You Want, by Harville Hendrix, Ph.D. (Harper and Row, 1988). Appendix contains communication exercises.

Trusting Ourselves, by Karen Johnson, M.D., and Tom Ferguson, M.D. (Atlantic Monthly Press, 1990). Well-researched guide to women's issues and problems. Communication section.

Opening Up: The Healing Power of Confiding in Others, by James W. Pennebaker (Avon Books, 1990). Why tell secrets and to whom.

Healing Conversations: What to Say When You Don't Know What to Say, by Nance Guilmartin (Josey-Bass, 2002). How to respond from the heart no matter what the circumstances.

Living a Connected Life: Creating and Maintaining Relationships That Last a Lifetime, by Kathleen A. Brehony (Owl Books, 2003). A well-written and well-researched look at creating and deepening the vital relationships that give life richness and meaning.

You Are What You Say, by Matthew Budd (Crown, 2000). A cogent overview of ontological theory and how it can change your life. Highly recommended.

WOMEN FOR COMFORT

What Is It?

An understanding look when you're having a bad day, an encircling arm holding you tight as you cry your pain away, the wonderful stillness in just being together. . . . The spirit of women together, comforting and caring for each other.

You'll Need:

Your journal and a pen.

A woman friend or two.

When to Do It:

- When you put nurturing friendships last on your to-do list.
- When you mistrust women.
- When you need to reconnect with a friend.

What to Do:

Remembering Friends

Sit down with your comfort journal. List every woman friend you can remember. Don't forget your best friend in third grade, the woman you traveled across Europe with, college roommates, the women who joined you in a pro-choice protest. Recognize the wealth of kind, strong women who have populated your life. Linger over your list, and feel the power of friendship.

Sketch a Story

Relax with one or more women friends. In turn, each woman lights a candle and relates her ultimate fantasy life. Pull from deep within yourself your personal dream. Get wild, be silly, there are no obstacles. Mention your surroundings, who shares this life with you, all the details. (My stories include being a mermaid queen and a famous art photographer.)

Valuing the Woman's Voice

The more we hear and see women who are successful at what they do, whether that success be a corporate presidency or weaving a beautiful rug, the more we value a woman's voice and

---

Remembering friends
Sketch a story
Valuing the woman's voice
Form a support club
A dream wheel
Support women

the more we will dissolve the fallacy of female inferiority. (Don't believe for a minute this myth has disappeared.)

One way to value our voice is to gather together a group of friends and celebrate successful women. Ask each woman to bring a story about a woman who has been successful in birthing and living her dream. It is great if everyone can bring something to show: a photograph, an example of her chosen woman's artwork, whatever is possible. Sit in a circle and have each woman talk about her subject's struggles and accomplishments. When everyone is finished, go around the circle again and discuss how these women can become role models and what aspects of which women you might emulate.

Form a Support Club

See "Creating a Comfort Network" and "Spirit Succor: Spiritual Nurturing with Others" for ideas on how to get a group together.

Forge a commitment with a few friends to meet regularly and support each other in a common pursuit. A support club can be a safe place to just complain about life, or you could discuss your common passions, like reading or gardening. You could get together for a wine-tasting class or an investing seminar; share the pain of divorce or the struggles of having a newborn baby. It could also be as simple as a regular commitment to spend time together. Or try a weekly women's topical discussion, choosing a new topic (personal or political) for each meeting. The point is to have a safe and dependable haven. To achieve this, each support club member needs to make a serious commitment to meeting. Be creative about where and when. The commitment is what matters.

A Dream Wheel

This idea was inspired by Hallie Iglehart's book *Womanspirit: A Guide to Women's Wisdom*.

Sharing dreams with other women helps us to connect with the power that exists beyond our logical mind. It is also a special way to forge an intimate bond among women friends.

Invite a few friends to spend the night together. Choose a place to sleep where everyone can lie together, forming the spokes of a wheel, with heads toward the center.

Structure the evening around dreams. Read from dream books, talk about the role of dreams in ancient cultures, and most importantly, decide what the dream goals are for tonight. You may all try to dream a solution to a particular problem facing one of you, or you may wish to just see what comes up. Have writing and drawing materials readily available for the morning.

Wake up quietly. Write or draw your dream. When everyone is done, go around the wheel sharing your dreams. Each woman listens closely. Questions and discussions should be reserved until the telling is complete.

Sometimes the wheel sleeping arrangement brings powerfully related dreams. If this is the case, discuss what you can do to honor the collective dream. An example could be visiting the ocean because each woman dreamed of it. The point is if the energy generated from your dreams feels potent and interrelated, take a little time at the end of the morning to create a connection between your everyday life and the dreams. It is a dynamic way to make the connection between the dreamers and to draw sustained energy from the dream message.

Support Women

Do whatever you can to help other women help themselves. Give time, money, and expertise to groups that help women. Educate yourself about women's place in society. Read prowomen magazines and books by prowomen authors. See films directed by women. Support women-run businesses. A very large network is available. Support and nurture others while you allow others to support and nurture you.

RESOURCES:

1,001 Things Everyone Should Know About Women's History, by Constance Jones (Main Street Books, 2000). Oh, the things you may not know!

Backlash: The Undeclared War Against American Women, by Susan Faludi (Anchor, 1992). The classic impeccably researched study of how feminism has been rejected by American culture.

The Tending Instinct, by Shelley E. Taylor (Owl Books, 2003). Why are we driven to seek relationship and tend others, even at a huge cost to ourselves?

The Red Tent, by Anita Diamant (Picador, 1998). Diamant's imagining of ancient female life in Jacob's clan.

Reinventing Ourselves After Motherhood: How Former Career Women Refocus Their Personal and Professional Lives After the Birth of a Child, by Susan Lewis (Contemporary, 2000). Covers issues from reidentifying yourself with peers to adjusting to changes in the relationship with your spouse.

The Dance of Deception: Pretending and Truth-Telling in Women's Lives, by Harriet G. Lerner (Quill, 1997). Unravels the ways (and whys) that we show the false and hide the real—even to our own selves. Brilliant.

A *Woman's Journey to God: Finding the Feminine Path*, by Joan Borysenko (Riverhead Books, 1999). Using samplings from various religious traditions, we learn women are intrinsically mystical and have been journeying toward God since the beginning of time.

COMFORT CARDS

What Is It?

Comfort cards are small messages of encouragement and aid you send to friends, friends send to you, and you send to yourself.

With a comfort card, you can easily help a friend, no matter how busy you are, and vice versa. And as miniature dollops of self-love, comfort cards lend themselves to delightful surprises, akin to finding a twenty-dollar bill in your jacket pocket.

You'll Need:

Postcards and three-by-five or larger index cards. Decorative postcards are a nice variation.

Stamps and a pen.

When to Do It:

- When you see challenging or depressing times ahead for yourself.
- When a friend is having a hard time.
- Whenever you or someone you care for is blue, overworked, or in need of a little comfort.

What to Do:

Composing a Comfort Card

When writing a card to a friend, offer only straightforward support and acceptance. Leave out criticisms and advice. When writing to yourself, still your critical voice and allow your nurturing voice to encourage and support you.

You might paste cartoons or jokes onto the cards. A pertinent quote would be another empathetic touch.

A Stockpile of Self-Cheer

When you are in a good mood, create a stockpile of happiness for rough times ahead. Jot positive thoughts and feelings about yourself on index cards. Hide these cards in scattered places, both obscure and obvious. You'll find them days, weeks, or even years later, just when you need them.

For example, tuck a comfort card in your spare tire to find when you get a flat. Or in the pages of a book you reach for when gloomy. Or in the

---

pocket of a suit jacket you'll wear when entertaining your boss. Slip a card into a research file you'll refer to months from now, when you're deep into a big project. Tailor the cards to each situation. For example, "I know I can handle this project. I'm doing a great job. I am proud of myself for everything I've done so far, and I now remind myself to take good care of myself so I can finish this project on time and successfully."

See "Ease into Comforting Yourself" for an explanation of affirmations.

For a variation, add affirmations to your card. When I was ill, I hid cards around the house that said things like, "I am now healthy and strong," "I love my body," and "I can now walk without a limp." They helped!

Encouragement from Friends

Imagine you have just had a baby. Every day for a few weeks, two or three friends give you postcards, telling you the endless sleeping and crying and feeding will end and that you will have a waistline again. Some comfort cards arrive in the mail; others are hidden around your house by a visiting friend to find later.

To count on comfort cards from friends, you can write, address, and stamp the cards yourself, then give them to close friends to mail either at their discretion or when you ask them to. Another way is to pick a friend or two and together come up with an informal plan for sending comfort cards to each other.

And, of course, comfort cards can be as simple as sending a hurting friend a warm postcard. Just don't do it with the expectation your friend will reciprocate someday. If you want comfort back, you will need to ask for it.

RESOURCES:

See "Reminding Yourself: Resources" for meditation books (source for quotes and wise, pithy statements) and "Get Silly: Resources" for humor books (cartoons and jokes).

The New Quotable Woman (Running Press, 2003). Crisp, funny, and laconic quotes by notable women.

Power Thought Cards, by Louise L. Hay (Hay House, 1999). Whimsically illustrated affirmation cards; helpful if you are having difficulty creating your own.

Self-Care Cards, by Cheryl Richardson (Hay House, 2001). Beautifully illustrated deck of self-care reminders.

Tips for Daily Living Cards: A Fifty-Card Deck, by Iyanla Vanzant (Hay House, 2003). Another beautifully illustrated deck; each card features a thought-provoking question and empowering suggestions.

Spiritual Rx: Prescriptions for Living a Meaningful Life, by Frederic Brussat and Mary Ann Brussat (Hyperion, 1996). Wide and deep collection of spiritual writings on different themes.

Websites:

Ze-Card
http://www.ze-card.com

Comfortqueen.com
http://comfortqueen.com/cards.html

A DAY OFF

What Is It?

A day off is an opportunity to set aside your routine, to take a miniature vacation. A day off is a chance to turn that wonderful nurturing power you possess toward someone who deeply needs it: You!

What It Isn't:

It is not about taking a day off to catch up on work at home. It is not about bill paying or errands. It is not about pleasing someone else. When you take a day off with your significant other, you both have things you want to do. That is a different experience. You can share your day off, but it must remain your day, governed solely by your needs and wishes.

You'll Need:

Your journal and a pen.

Whatever you need to help you relax and have fun.

When to Do It:

- When you can't remember the last time you took an entire day off.
- When you feel like you have three-day-old coffee, instead of blood, in your veins, and no matter how much you sleep you are still exhausted.
- When you hunger for a new perspective, a jolt of creative fun.

What to Do:

Retreat Fantasy

Get away to a quiet spot, keeping your comfort journal and pen nearby. Ask yourself:

If you had twenty-four hours

in which to do anything,

be anywhere, with anyone,

what would you do?

Retreat fantasy
Make a picnic
Make a bliss list
Tourist for a day
Reconnect with someone special
A just-being day
A fantasy day
A silent day
Trouble?

Close your eyes and let your mind go wild! Push yourself to transcend ordinary space, time, and monetary restrictions. What do you genuinely want to do?

Open your eyes and write your thoughts in your comfort journal. Don't censor yourself because you know you could never afford it or because people cannot fly.

My fantasy is to "rent a house on the north coast of California and fill it with plenty of food (fresh baked bread, Florida lobster, Toblerone chocolate, baked potatoes, and Piper-Sonoma champagne). Everyone I love would be there for a few hours, then suddenly it would be just me, my husband, and my dog. We would walk on the beach in the cold and fog, then my husband and I would take a bubble bath surrounded by candles. Afterward, we would eat fresh lobster and talk and listen to each other, in front of a cozy fire."

Look at your fantasy. What elements could you incorporate into your day off? Expand your horizons. Your day off can be a lot more than browsing in the mall or lunch with a friend.

Make a Picnic

Have you ever packed a picnic, a nice picnic, just for yourself?

Make a Bliss List

Take your day off to name and contemplate your passions. Here is my list:

Gardening, Fortnum and Mason tea, sushi, rainy days in bed reading, chocolate, *Stuart Little* by E. B. White, Big Sur, a fall day in the New Hampshire woods, my best friend Barbra, any meal my friend Nikki makes, women's rights, white water canoeing.

See "Comfort Journal: Investigate What Being Good to Yourself Means" for additional help.

Tourist for a Day

Drive to a nearby town or a strange part of your city that you have always wanted to explore. Spend the day. Visit a bookstore, drink a cup of tea in a café. Let yourself be a stranger. Immerse yourself in a different culture. Get a glimpse of life outside your territory. Open yourself to that feeling of newness, of someplace different.

Reconnect with Someone Special

See "Women for Comfort: Remembering Friends."

Plan to spend part of your day with a truly wonderful person with whom you've lost touch. Tell your special person that this is your day off and that you would be honored if they would share part of it with you.

A Just-Being Day

See "Ease into Comforting Yourself."

No clocks, no schedules. Eat whatever you want whenever you are hungry. Nap if you want. Go to sleep at six or at midnight. Celebrate that you are you, alive and totally unique.

A Fantasy Day

See "Becoming a Guru of Play" and "Get Silly."

Read poetry and fairy tales. Rent a fantasy movie. Play dress-up. Visit a place in your town that piques your private imagination; try a wax museum, shadowy antique store, or art gallery.

A Silent Day

See "Solitude: Silent Solitude."

Arrange your life so you don't have to speak for a day. Afterward, record your experiences and insights in your journal. Perhaps being without words will liberate you to hear your inner needs and wants more clearly.

Trouble?

See "A Self-Care Schedule: How to Rescue Time for Self-Nurturing" and "Creative Selfishness: Say No."

If the idea of taking a whole day off sends you into tremors, start with a half day. If you find yourself doing chores or giving up your plans to take care of someone else's problem on your day off, that's okay. Just notice what you are doing, and try again soon to take a day off just for you.

RESOURCES:

Ecstasy, by Robert A. Johnson (HarperSanFrancisco, 1987). About the nature of ecstasy and how to reconnect with the ecstatic element that lies dormant in each of us.

Flow: The Psychology of Optimal Experience, by Mihaly Csikszentmihalyi (Perennial, 1993). A study of optimal experiences with examples of how life can be made more enjoyable.

Twenty-Minute Retreats: Revive Your Spirit in Just Minutes a Day with Simple Self-Led Practices, by Rachel Harris (Owl Books, 2000). Wonderful, simple, varied meditations.

A New Adventure Every Day: 541 Simple Ways to Live with Pizzazz, by David Silberkleit (Sourcebooks, 2002). Simple, fun activities perfect to try on a day off or to incorporate into your everyday life.

14,000 Things to Be Happy About, by Barbara Ann Kipfer (Workman Publishing, 1990). A classic, comprehensive Bliss List to inspire you to create your own.

Inner Outings: The Diarist's Deck of Thirty-three Cards and Book of Exploration, by Charlene Geiss and Claudia Jessup (New World Library, 2002). Lovely deck of illustrated cards corresponding to activities and writing exercises ideal for an introspective day off.

A Big New Free Happy Unusual Life: Self-Expression and Spiritual Practice for Those Who Have Time for Neither, by Nina Wise (Broadway Books, 2002). Brief exercises to nurture spirituality and creativity, wonderful for easing into a day off.

365 Health and Happiness Boosters, by M. J. Ryan (Conari Press, 2000). Simple, concrete ideas and activities to help you experience more joy.

HIDING UNDER THE COVERS

What Is It?

Hiding under the covers is a planned retreat, a healthy way to baby yourself. Give yourself permission to stay in bed or on the couch for a day, and do whatever you like. That may be sleeping, reading, eating, watching old black and white movies, or a combination of all these. This may sound indulgent, but it isn't!

Hiding under the covers is a variation of playing sick. Remember when you were a child and you would stay home from school, sick enough not to feel guilty, but not so sick you couldn't enjoy the Jell-O your mom made or *Leave It to Beaver*? That is the warm, safe feeling you need to recreate.

Allowing yourself to retreat gives you the critical time you need to reflect on your life and balance yourself. By taking time for yourself in such a lavish way, you are saying to your mind and body, "I deserve the same amount of love and care I give to others."

You'll Need:

Your bed or couch.

Fluffy blankets and lots of pillows.

Snack food, books, magazines. Whatever fun and totally silly things make you feel good.

When to Do It:

- When you are so burned out you can barely keep going.
- When you keep saying to yourself, "I'll just power through this," or "If I just keep my feet moving," or "Once I'm finished with this project, I can rest."
- When you've been fighting a cold or have been having a lot of headaches.
- When you've been feeling moderately depressed and you don't know why.
- When you never allow yourself to just lie around and relax.

Banish guilt!	*Munchies*
Arrange your hiding space	*Hiding out beauty*
Screen your calls	*Television*
Scent the room	*Again and again*
Literary fun	*A whole day isn't necessary (although it is nice)*

What to Do:

Banish Guilt!

The key to getting comfort from hiding under the covers is to give yourself permission to take time off and crawl into bed *without berating yourself*. A good way to do that is to turn off your annoying inner critic. The inner critic may say things like, "You can't do this; people are depending on you." "Sleeping, in the middle of the day? What will you sink to next?" "What a wimp! In my day. . . ."

Gently tell yourself with your nurturing voice that by taking a day off and allowing yourself to be blue or tired you are performing a very important duty. You will be better to others, more effective at your job, and a more enjoyable person to live with if you take time out.

See "Your Nurturing Voice" and "Creative Selfishness: Eliminate Guilt."

Arrange Your Hiding Space

Make the space where you plan to spend the day as comfortable as possible. That may mean blobbing out on the couch, under a heap of cuddly blankets. Or hide your partner's dirty socks, make the bed with clean sheets, and stock your bedside table with hot cinnamon tea and sourdough toast. Whatever appeals to *you*.

Screen Your Calls

Turn on your answering machine or unplug the phone. Talk only to people who help you feel better. Avoid all unnurturing people.

See "Creating a Comfort Network."

Scent the Room

Hide a couple of sachets between the blankets.

See "Sweet Scents" for more ideas.

Bake cookies.

Open the windows and let in fresh air.

Put a freesia or rose in a bud vase on your nightstand.

HIDING UNDER THE COVERS

See "Reading like a Child" for more ideas.

Literary Fun

Immerse yourself in a good or distracting novel. Browse in a bookstore and stock up on a few titles to tuck away for your next day off. A few of my favorite hiding-out books are *Animal Dreams* by Barbara Kingslover, *A Winter's Tale* by Mark Helprin, *Middlemarch* by George Eliot, *The Baron in the Trees* by Italo Calvino, and *To Kill a Mockingbird* by Harper Lee.

Munchies

See "When I Think of Comfort, I Think of Food."

Create a tray of food to have in bed. Consider an attractive place mat and your prettiest dishes. Try a bowl of grapes, a raspberry tart, or a few chocolates—whatever your body craves.

Hiding Out Beauty

You may feel like doing a beauty regimen. Or you may banish mirrors and makeup for the day. Follow your impulse.

Television

Watching television on your hiding time can be good or it can be bad. Long hours in front of daytime TV can end up making you feel more tired and stressed than before. But if you never get to watch daytime TV, maybe that is just what you need.

If you have a VCR, get into the habit of taping old movies to watch on these mental health days. Renting a familiar film can be very comforting. My favorites are *E.T.*, *Field of Dreams*, *A Room with a View*, *Annie Hall*, *Bagdad Cafe*, *Princess Bride*, *The Women*, and *The Philadelphia Story*.

Again and Again

Practice makes perfect. Take a hiding-out day to see what you need to feel refreshed and renewed. Follow your desires. Indulge yourself.

A Whole Day Isn't Necessary (Although It Is Nice)

You don't have to hide for an entire day. An hour or two on a Saturday morning, leaving work early, skipping a dinner party you didn't want to go to. . . . The options are endless.

RESOURCES:

Everyone's Mandala Coloring Book, by Monique Mandali (Falcon, 1994). A series of healing mandalas for you to color.

Booklust, by Nancy Pearl (Sasquatch Books, 2003). Pearl is probably our nation's most famous librarian. Reading for every mood, moment, and reason!

Bibliotherapy: The Girl's Guide to Books for Every Phase of Our Lives, by Nancy K. Peske and Beverly West (Dell, 2001). Categorized by mood.

Cinematherapy: The Girl's Guide to Movies for Every Mood, by Nancy K. Peske and Beverly West (Dell, 1999). Bibliotherapy for movies.

Simple Pleasures: Soothing Suggestions and Small Comforts for Living Well Year Round, by Robert Taylor, Susannah Seton, and David Greer (Gramercy, 2000). Collection of stories and ideas.

1,001 Ways to Relax: An Illustrated Guide to Reducing Stress, by Mike George (Chronicle Books, 2004). Relaxing ideas and activities.

Bedtime Stories: A Unique Guided Relaxation Program for Falling Asleep and Entering the World of Dreams, by Clarissa Pinkola Estes, Ph.D. (Sounds True, 2002). Be read to as if you were a child.

Music:

Velveteen Rabbit by George Winston and Meryl Streep, *On a Starry Night: Lullabies* by various artists

Websites:

The Internet Movie Database
http://www.imdb.com

Notable Books: The List for America's Readers
www.ala.org

BECOMING A GURU OF PLAY

What Is It?

When we were children, we knew how to genuinely have fun. We were intimately in touch with our senses. We could spend hours playing make-believe with a box or exploring the backyard. Reactivating those wonderful feelings of childlike enjoyment and reconnecting with the part of us that is still a child creates a deep soul comfort that is crucial for our happiness and well-being.

You'll Need:

Various playthings. Soap bubbles and trees, shadows and dogs, whatever is handy and enticing.

When to Do It:

- When you've been grinding your teeth at night.
- When you are restless and the last thing you want to do is watch TV.
- When you've been working every weekend.
- Whenever you need to comfort the part of you that is still a small child, aching for love, attention, and *fun!*

What to Do:

Simple Games

Play with soap bubbles. Watch shadows dance on the wall. Play jacks. Finger paint and get really messy. Color in a coloring book.

Water Rollicks

Play in the rain. Play with a garden hose. Play tag with lawn sprinklers. Play with water in the bathtub or ocean. Slide in the mud. Make mud pies. Dribble water on paper and then trace the design with markers. Have a squirt gun fight with a friend.

Tastes, Textures, and Tones

Absorb the quiet of snow falling at night. Suck on a peppermint or squash a caramel in your mouth. Put on crazy music and move. Make sounds using your nose as a musical instrument.

Hugs

Hug a dog. Hug a tree. Hug someone you love, really hard.

Move Your Body

Skip. Jump rope. Turn a somersault. Throw a Frisbee. Roller-skate on a sidewalk. Roll down a grassy hill.

See "Body Delights" for more ideas.

Play Dress-Up

Wear a mask. Have a costume party. Paint faces on your toenails.

Field Trips

Go to the zoo. Go to a park and swing on the swings. Find a secret place to hide for a half hour.

Fun Things

Watch cartoons. Buy a comic book. Make a plaster hand print. Find a friend and draw each other's silhouettes. Have a food fight with marshmallows. Watch fireworks light up the sky. Escape to a matinee.

Natural Antics

Dig in the dirt. Press flowers. Go for a long walk in wet grass in your bare feet. Make mud pies. Make a sand castle, then smash it.

Be Silly

See "Get Silly" for more possibilities.

Celebrate Tuesdays. Wear a tall black top hat to do errands. Put on a disguise, go visit your neighbor, and act completely normal.

For the Greatest Childlike Comfort

Bake cookies and eat them warm, with cold milk.

RESOURCES:

How to Eat Like a Child, by Delia Ephron (Viking Press, 1977). Inspiration to help you feel childlike.

Free Play: Improvisation in Life and Art, by Stephen Nachmanovitch (Jeremy Tarcher, 1991). This is the book to read to convince yourself you need to play.

Permission to Play: Taking Time to Renew Your Smile, by Jill Murphy Long (Sourcebooks Trade, 2003). Encouragement, ideas, and activities to incorporate play into your life.

Pencil Dancing: New Ways to Free Your Creative Spirit, by Mari Messer (Walking Stick Press, 2001). A hands-on guide to enlarging your creative perspective through wonder and play.

Websites:

Tera Leigh
http://www.teraleigh.com

Camp Sark
http://www.campsark.com

Be Real Magazine
http://www.berealmag.com

Artella Words and Art
http://www.artellawordsandart.com

READING LIKE A CHILD

What Is It?

Reading children's books is a simple but very effective way to comfort ourselves. We can reconnect with innocence, magic, and hope.

Take a break from your daily struggles and worries to escape into the familiar world of a beloved story or to explore a book you never read as a child. Reconnect with wonder, and comfort the part of yourself that is still a child.

You'll Need:

Children's books.

When to Do It:

- When your life feels flat and gray.
- When you need a fresh perspective on a problem and entering into the viewpoint of a child might help.
- When you long to be with your parents but that is impossible.
- When your imagination needs recharging.

What to Do:

Explore like a Child

Visit a children's bookstore. Considerably comforting places in their own right, they are filled with a wide selection of tantalizing titles. Look at the exquisite illustrations, and inhale the clean smell of crisp, new pages.

You may be surprised by how familiar your bookseller will be with the sight of an adult searching for a long-forgotten title. Don't be ashamed to ask for help.

Explore like a child *Libraries are great too*

Look for books you loved as a child. I get great comfort out of unearthing old favorites, like *Harriet the Spy* by Louise Fitzhugh, *The Phantom Tollbooth* by Norton Juster, or *The Wolves of Willoughby Chase* by Joan Chase. Look for classics you never got to read, like *The Secret Garden* by Frances Hodgson Burnett or *The Wind in the Willows* by Graham Swift.

Libraries Are Great Too

Almost every child has spent time in a library, doing research for school projects, taking out books for a long weekend. Take some time to wander through the children's section of your library. Take in the atmosphere, sit in one of the little chairs, watch the children around you reading.

If you feel silly, pretend you are looking for books for your children or your niece.

RESOURCES:

Any of the Olivia books by *New Yorker* artist Ian Falconer. Sophisticated picture books hilarious enough to delight even the most reluctant adult.

Any of the Ramona books by Beverly Cleary. Sweeps you back to childhood's joys and tribulations in a comforting safety net of humor and warmth.

Inner Child Cards: A Fairy-Tale Tarot, by Isha Lerner and Mark Lerner (Bear and Co., 2001). Beautifully illustrated version of the traditional tarot deck, incorporating fairy-tale archetypes to aid in healing your inner child.

Websites:

On-Lion for Kids! (Children's Section of the New York Public Library) http://www.nypl.org

The American Library Association's Notable Children's Books List http://www.ala.org (click on "Libraries & You" to get to the children's list)

GET SILLY

What Is It?

Laughter is healing, helpful, and playful. Did you know your brain secretes antidepressant biochemicals when you laugh? Being able to laugh at yourself, act silly, or tell a joke can provide much-needed comfort in anxious or sad situations. A good laugh when you're depressed can help you gain the relief and perspective you may desperately need.

You'll Need:

Your sense of humor.

A little courage.

Funny movies, videos, books, cartoons, comedy recordings, old photographs.

When to Do It:

- When you find yourself taking life very seriously.
- When you often find yourself wanting to laugh or quip a joke but are afraid of what people will think.

What to Do:

Be a Funny Person

Impersonate a happy-go-lucky person for a day. Think of an entertainer or a character who is funny, easygoing, and always ready with a quip. Be Lily Tomlin, Bette Midler, Lucille Ball, or someone in your own life whom you find funny. Throughout your day, ask yourself, "How would that person react to this situation?"

Playful Props

Carry a jar of bubbles in your car. Add a little fantasy to the next traffic jam.

Next time a salesperson rings your doorbell, answer it wearing pop-out eyeglasses or a paper mask of the pope.

Try wearing a fake plastic nose that resembles a parrot or an elephant when meeting a depressed friend for dinner.

About to snap off your mate's head? Slip a pair of Groucho glasses on first. Just try being cranky while wearing these glasses!

Be a funny person	*Nonsense*
Playful props	*Exaggerate*
Party humor	*Surround yourself with buffoonery*

Party Humor

Organize a silly party. Have friends prepare jokes, gags, excerpts from favorite humor books to read aloud. Play a funny scene from a classic comedy film. Wear goofy little hats. Recite favorite Monty Python routines. Eat pickles, marshmallows, Jell-O, and miniature hot dogs.

Nonsense

See "Becoming a Guru of Play" for inspiring silliness.

Add malarkey to your life. Jump out of bed tomorrow morning and pretend you are a monkey. Assume absurd postures while blow-drying your hair. Hoot and howl on the way to work.

Turn a somersault at the mall.

Dye your hair purple for a day. (Beauty supply or costume shops carry wash-out sprays.)

Paint your dog's toenails red.

Wear hats for each job you do: a chef's hat, a chauffeur's cap, a bandanna.

Wear false eyelashes or different-colored socks and see who notices.

Wave at people you don't know.

On a toll bridge, pay the toll for the person behind you.

Exaggerate

Things are awful, right? The world stinks, your life is meaningless, your job is awful, you're afraid to ask for a raise, you'll never get out of this one-horse town. Get into it! Slump, whine, crawl on the floor, curse, wallow in your self-pity. Throw a tantrum. Be a baby. Let out all your negative feelings and beliefs. Why is this funny? Because if you throw a real stinker, if you complain and sulk like nobody's business, you will feel ten pounds lighter, full of new energy, and you won't be able to keep a straight face.

Try sharing this exercise with coworkers who are under equal pressure or with your partner before the holidays or with your pet.

See "Animal Antidotes."

Surround Yourself with Buffoonery

Create a bulletin board plastered with cartoons, pictures, silly buttons, bumper stickers, and funny stories. Rearrange and add to it often. Display it in a prominent place.

Start a humor file. Store it near your mortgage file or next to a current project file. You'll bump into it in times of need.

Start a library of funny books, videos, and comedy recordings. Borrow from the library or trade with friends to keep the variety going. Listen to a Woody Allen tape in your car. Keep a *Calvin and Hobbes* book in your desk drawer for a laugh break. Expose yourself to types of humor and comedians you've never experienced. On a good day, juice up your supply of what you like. Make laughter easily available for ready comfort during down times.

You know that tomorrow you are going to come home late and exhausted. Before bed, cue up a favorite comedy show or movie in your VCR. Place popcorn in the microwave, get your fuzzy robe out, and prop your favorite stuffed animal or blanket on the couch. The next night, you walk in the door, and presto, instant humorous comfort.

RESOURCES:

Costume and magic shops, garage sales, and thrift stores are chock-full of inexpensive props.

Life's a Stitch: The Best of Contemporary Women's Humor, edited by Anne Safran Dalin (Random House, 2002). Anthology of humorous stories, poems, cartoons, and more from well-known female writers; royalties and a percentage of the proceeds are donated to the American Foundation for

AIDS Research, the National Coalition Against Domestic Violence, and the National Alliance of Breast Cancer Organizations.

Fifty-two Silly Things to Do When You Are Blue, by Lynn Gordon (Chronicle Books, 1994). Illustrated deck of cards featuring simple activities to encourage playfulness and spontaneity.

Dave Barry's Greatest Hits, by Dave Barry (Columbine Trade, 1991). A collection of the Pulitzer Prize–winning humorist's best columns.

Any of the *Calvin and Hobbes* collections by Bill Watterson.

Any of the *Far Side* collections by Gary Larson.

Any of the *Sylvia* collections by Nicole Hollander.

Any of the *Peanuts* collections by Charles Schulz.

Websites:

Found Objects
http://www.foundobjects.com

Cool Animal Stuff
http://www.coolanimalstuff.com

Diddams Party Stores
http://www.diddams.com

Funny Times
http://www.funnytimes.com

World Laughter
http://www.worldlaughter.com

The Onion
http://www.onion.com

Storypeople
http://www.storypeople.com

Archie McPhee
http://www.mcphee.com

News of the Weird
http://www.newsoftheweird.com

ANIMAL ANTIDOTES

What Is It?

Animals are wonderful sources of comfort. We can be as needy, whiny, depressed, or out of sorts as we want, and our pets still love us. Dogs, cats, birds, even fish offer a boundless supply of solace that many medical studies have found can help you live a longer and healthier life.

You'll Need:

An animal of any kind. If you don't own any pets, don't worry. Keep reading.

When to Do It:

- When you need some unconditional love.
- When you need to touch life.
- When you have been cooped up in a city or barren office building for what seems like your entire life.

What to Do:

Get a Pet

If you already have one or two or ten, skip to the next section. If you are considering getting a pet, realize what a massive commitment this is and exactly how it will affect your life. I wouldn't trade my dog for anything in the world, but I sometimes resent the restrictions and compromises that having him causes.

Borrowing pets is one solution. This can help you decide if you want one and give you some furry love if you are too busy for a full-time commitment or live in a place that doesn't allow pets. Try pet-sitting for friends. Put a sign in a vet's office offering to sit for a dog or cat. Borrow an animal from a friend for a day. Arrange with a private pound to baby-sit a dog or cat over a lonely holiday weekend.

Birds, fish, lizards, and iguanas require less care than traditional animals, and they are usually allowed in apartments. Although they are hard to cuddle, they do bring life into your home.

The next two exercises were sparked by *The Four-Footed Therapist* by animal lover and therapist Janet Rupert.

Relax like an Animal

Lie down on the floor beside your animal friend, pretend a beloved pet is lying beside you, or picture a wild animal relaxing in her natural habitat.

Close your eyes and **relax.** Feel yourself becoming your animal. Go inside its skin. You are now as free, as calm, as in-the-moment as this animal naturally is.

When you are ready, open your eyes and imitate your animal. How is he or she lying? Sprawled out, totally tranquil? Imitate this total abandon. Is your cat prowling around the room, jumping at shadows and breezes? Do this. Scratch, purr, stretch out in the sun. Perhaps you are imagining an otter gliding gracefully downriver? Feel the cool water sliding past you. Imagine what it feels like to be that playful, supple, and curious. Eat like your animal. Imitate the growls and yowls. Animals don't have jobs, deadlines, or bills. Allow yourself to feel happy and carefree. Let yourself go.

When you feel you've been animal-like long enough, collapse on the floor, close your eyes, and bask in your feelings of natural peace. If appropriate, hug your pet.

Unconditional Love

Lie down and hug a pet you care for. Stroke its fur. Observe how much love you give to this animal. Talk to this animal. Tell it all the things you love about it. Look into your animal's eyes, and see how good it feels to be loved so totally. Keep stroking your animal while closing your eyes. Imagine that some of the unconditional love you are feeling for this animal is traveling up through your fingers, into your hand, along your arm, and deep into your own heart. You feel a warm glow. You are loved.

Continue stroking your animal. Think back to a very happy time. It could be from your childhood, teenage years, perhaps only a few days ago—any time you felt totally loved, appreciated, full of the unique life force that makes you *you*. Relate this memory to your pet. Tell your animal in detail how wonderful you felt, what made you so happy, how things looked, smelled, even tasted during that happy time.

Keep stroking your pet. Feel once more the connection of unconditional love between you and this animal. Realize you can reestablish this connection any time you need it. Give your animal one more big hug, and open your eyes.

Nurture Your Pet Along with Yourself

Buy your cat catnip and yourself some Swiss almond decaf coffee.

Stuffed animals also make good furry friends. Design a day off around selecting your new pet. Treat yourself to a healthy lunch, some solitude, perhaps a nap afterward with your new animal. You could choose different stuffed animals for different functions in your life: a teddy bear to sleep with, a toad to talk to in the bathroom, a pig to cheer you up at work.

Take your dog to obedience school.

Go on a picnic with your friend and her dog. Bring a rawhide for the dog and a delicious supper for the humans. Lie in the sun afterward, and imitate the dog's total relaxation.

Exercise like an animal. Pretend you are a gazelle when running or a bear when lifting weights.

Animal Activism

Get comfort from helping animals in need. Join Greenpeace. Donate time to a local pound. Consider checking to be sure the beauty and household products you are using are cruelty free (meaning they don't use animals in testing).

RESOURCES:

Greenpeace, 1436 U Street NW, Washington, DC 20009. http://www.greenpeace.org

Love, Miracles, and Animal Healing, by Allen M. Schoen, D.V.M., and Pam Proctor (Fireside, 1996). A book about the spiritual bonding between animals and humans.

What Animals Can Teach Us About Spirituality, by Diana Guerrero (Skylight Paths, 2003). A look toward the animal kingdom for a spiritual mentor. Tools, methods, and examples designed to give you a better understanding of animals. Animals know how to live in the now, where the past is gone and future yet to come.

Dogs That Know When Their Owners Are Coming Home: And Other Unexplained Powers of Animals, by Rupert Sheldrake (Three Rivers Press, 2000). Investigates pets' psychic powers and seemingly paranormal abilities.

A Dog Year: Twelve Months, Four Dogs, and Me, by Jon Katz (Random House, 2003). The connection between a man and his dogs, funny at times, sad at others.

The Beginner's Guide to Animal Communication, by Carol Gurney (Sounds True Audio, 2000). For anyone seeking a "heart-to-heart" connection with the special companions in their lives.

GREEN THINGS

What Is It?

Working with plants, studying colorful gardening and bulb catalogs, strolling through a fragrant arboretum: what a calming, refreshing, life-affirming way to comfort yourself! A time-honored and healthy tradition of self-nurturing can be found in growing and appreciating plants and flowers.

You'll Need:

Seed-starter soil, potting dirt, pots, cardboard egg cartons, and an outside area.

Seeds, seedlings, bulbs, and/or houseplants.

Water and plentiful sunlight.

A trowel or hand spade is useful.

When to Do It:

- When you can't remember the last time you touched anything green.
- When you come home from work and need to unwind but you aren't sure what to do instead of flicking on the TV or pouring yourself a drink.
- If you are always drawn to gardening books in the bookstore or country living books but are overwhelmed by the idea of growing anything.

What to Do:

A Seed Garden

Next time you need a mildly ambitious project, head for a local nursery or browse through a seed catalog for some tiny miracles. Easy-to-grow seed choices include bush-type sweet peas, impatiens, morning glories, cosmos, nasturtiums, forget-me-nots, and all kinds of sunflowers. Fill small clay or plastic pots (with drainage holes) or cardboard egg cartons (plastic doesn't breathe) with seed-starter soil. Moisten thoroughly with water. Sprinkle your seeds over the surface, press lightly with your fingertips, and enclose the containers in a clear plastic bag.

Choose a warm, sheltered location for your seeds. (My favorite place is the top of my gas range, which is always warm. The top of the dryer is another idea.) You are now guaranteed engrossing, but not overwhelming, daily solace as you tend to your seed babies. Keep them moist by watering every other day or so. Watch for their tiny green heads to unfurl. When you see sprouts, remove the plastic bag. Thin according to seed packet directions. When the seedlings are large enough, usually around three inches tall, transplant to a larger pot or into a sunny patch of earth.

More Dirt

The danger in playing with green things for comfort is that you will become overwhelmed or depressed if your projects don't work or become too large. Keep the scale small, and remember that nothing is at stake. You are not a pioneer woman who must feed her family from your one bean plant. Dig deep holes, make mud pies, let your mind be absorbed in the optimistic activities around you. Name your plants. I find that watering my plants is one of the most calming things I can do after a long day of writing. I also like to work out my anger by weeding or breaking up already-broken clay pots.

Houseplants

If you have always killed plants in the past, start with just two or three different plants. This gives you variety without overwhelming you. Easy houseplant choices include lipstick vine *(Aeschynanthus)* or rabbit's foot fern *(Davallia)* or corn plant *(Dracaena)* or Swedish ivy *(Plectranthus)*.

All of these plants like bright western or southern exposures with very little direct sunlight. Water evenly and regularly. Don't mist African violets *(Saintpaulia)* or snake plant *(Sansevieria)*, other easy-to-grow varieties.

Make a twice weekly ritual out of caring for your plants. Play music. Water, remove dead leaves or faded blossoms, mist, and rearrange plants for more or less light. I get comfort from talking to my plants, although when I do this in the front yard, people tend to stare.

Bulbs

This is easy and a great antidote for the winter blues. It sounds difficult, but once you try it, you'll do it every winter! Buy hyacinths, daffodils, narcissuses, crocuses, or tulips in October. Store for two months in the crisper of your refrigerator. In January, place bulbs in a pot or dish with pebbles, marbles, or rocks around them. (These just keep the bulb in place.) Water until the bulbs are almost covered. Place in a sunny (but not direct sun) location. Replenish the water every few days. They will bloom quickly and for a month or more.

Brown Thumbs

Nurture your green needs by visiting a particularly glorious florist shop. Linger over the flowers, sniff them, ask their names. Buy a single exquisite flower.

Collect a few small glass bottles, and arrange unusual blossoms in them. Keep a bottle on your desk, and when the day is going badly, stop and study the flower for a moment.

Sketch or do a watercolor (not for art but for yourself) of a poppy, a palm tree, a white rose.

Check out a few garden picture books from the library, sip fruit juice, and imagine yourself surrounded by flowers.

See "Nature's Solace" for related ideas.

See Nature's Solace for related ideas.

Visiting Gardens

On a day when you are not aching for comfort, research the gardens or parks open to the public in your area. The phone book, a university, a women's club, or a Junior League organization can help. You can also watch the papers for flower and gardening shows as well as historical house and garden tours.

Next time you pine for the tranquillity of nature, go to one of your prepicked garden places. As you enter the garden, stop. Consciously leave all your worries, burdens, and tensions at the entrance. Tell your critic they will be safe here until you return. If, during your wanderings in the garden, you begin to worry, send that worry back to keep the others company.

Study an orchid. Breathe deeply of the humid air inside a greenhouse. Stare into a reflecting pool. Meditate on a stone, imagining what it would be like to exist at that slow, prehistoric level. Step back and squint your eyes, reducing the gardens to Monet-like splashes of colors. Imagine that all the flowers, grasses, and trees are sending their vital energy straight into your heart!

RESOURCES:

Creating Eden: The Garden as a Healing Space, by Marilyn Barrett (HarperSanFrancisco, 1992). Meditations for the garden.

Growing Myself: A Spiritual Journey Through Gardening, by Judith Handelsman (Plume, 1997). Essays about gardening as a spiritual restorative.

Tending the Earth, Mending the Spirit: The Healing Gifts of Gardening, by Connie Goldman (Hazelden, 2000). Interviews with hundreds of famous gardeners on why they garden. Recovery slant.

Garden Retreats: Creating an Outdoor Sanctuary, by Barbara Blossom Ashmun, with photos by Allan Mandell (Chronicle Books, 2000). Gorgeous photos and practical guidance for creating an outdoor room of your own.

Tea Gardens: Places to Make and Take Tea, by Ann Lovejoy, with photos by Allan Mandell (Chronicle Books, 1998). Ann wrote the first garden book I ever understood garden design from. Years later, I'm her neighbor. Check out all her wonderful gardening books, especially if you live in the Northwest.

NATURE'S SOLACE

What Is It?

When I am completely fed up with life, I head for the hills. The most deeply nurturing and life-affirming experiences of my life have taken place in nature. Confronted by the beauty, the power, the mystery that can be found even in a nearby patch of woods, I loosen my white-knuckle hold on life and breathe a little slower, a little deeper.

Why is nature nurturing? Because touching the unspoiled inspires awe and hope in us. It gives us perspective. Nature feeds our creative spirits by surrounding us with mysteries that will never be knowable. If we walk in it long enough, the wilderness calms us, slowing us to its speed. Finally, nature is cleansing, washing away worries, fears, and self-doubts.

You'll Need:

Information about wild spaces near and far.

When to Do It:

- When you can't remember the last time you went to sleep with moonlight on your face or saw a deer grazing in the woods or grabbed the Earth and hugged it.
- If you live in a city or apartment building that allows you little contact with nature.
- If you loved nature adventures as a child but don't make time for them as an adult.

What to Do:

Prepare

Your nature getaway will be made much easier if, when you are in an energetic mood, you spend a little time researching information about nature sites near you. There are dozens of wonderful places near everyone, even city dwellers. Start a file filled with a variety of information, both for quick getaways and for more involved adventures. Look for cheap cabins in a national forest, canoeing on a mellow river, camping on a little-known island, hiking trails, hidden waterfalls, hot springs. Check bookstore and wilderness outfitting stores for local hiking and camping books. Ask friends.

Connect

This meditation was inspired by the work of Beverly Antaeus, a wilderness leader and writer working in New Mexico.

Next time you feel rotten, sluggish, or out of kilter, go to one of your nature areas. Find a place to lie down, directly on the ground. **Relax.** Close your eyes. Feel the stillness of the Earth under you. Feel its steady pulse.

Imagine the Earth is taking away your pain, sorrow, frustration, disappointments. Visualize these negative emotions and experiences leaving you and traveling down, down to the center of the Earth. See the molten core there. Imagine your feelings colliding with the pulsating, boiling, alive center of the Earth. Sparks fly, explosions sound. Out of the liquified center beams a ray of healing energy. You watch this energy streaming up, up through the strata of rock and fossils, past tree roots and rabbits curled in their burrows, until this energy reaches you. It radiates up from the ground and through the soles of your feet. Breathe in this primeval life force. Feel the Earth's vitality as it travels up your calves and thighs, courses through your buttocks and into your womb. It fills your stomach and lungs, expands your heart, flows through each arm, and lights up every one of your fingers. Up, up into your jaw and forehead. . . . And finally this pure energy illuminates your mind. You bask in this complete, wonderful, renewing warmth. This energy nourishes and feeds your entire being.

Now imagine the Earth's life force flowing out of your fingertips and toes, circling around and washing over you, then returning to the Earth. You are now part of the cycle of nature. Feel the steady, gentle pulse as this life force flows throughout your body, out your fingers and toes, and back down into the Earth. You are one with all of nature, you are connected to all that is alive.

Be part of this energy circle as long as you like. When you are completely at peace, filled with calm well-being, take one more deep, deep breath, creating a well of energy in your heart to draw from in the coming weeks. Thank the Earth. Know that you are forever part of the Earth and can return for sustenance anytime you wish.

Birthday Ritual

Every (or every other) year, try to make time for a nature-based birthday ritual. You could walk on the beach and immerse yourself in the sound of the water. You could pick vegetables and make a salad out of them. You could explore nature for objects that speak to you, like a smooth river stone or an eagle's feather, and take them home to study as a symbol for the coming year. The goal is to make a connection between your life cycle and the Earth's. This connection tends to go beyond words and into the realm of the spirit. Spend even a few minutes on your day of birth with nature, and see what happens.

Sleep in the Moonlight

A magical event! Try sleeping in the moonlight on your roof, in your backyard, in the middle of the desert, or on top of a mountain. Plan a trip with several close friends to camp out under a full moon. Make sure you bring a warm sleeping bag and an insulating mat.

Lie on your back, and watch the moon rise. Watch the stars, any clouds, the blackness around everything. Close your eyes, and compare the darkness around you with the darkness inside. Feel the vastness of space. Imagine the moon is bathing you in magical radiance. Perhaps you want to sing a song to the moon or dance a moonlight jig. This would be the perfect time to devise a ritual that addresses a present need.

Plan a Transformational Wilderness Retreat

Abscond with several close friends into nature, and allow the Earth to invade your dreams. Keep safety in mind! If you are not experienced with the wilds, take someone who is. Wilderness, especially mountain, conditions can change radically in a matter of minutes. Plan and pack accordingly.

See "Women for Comfort: A Dream Wheel"; "Courage Rituals: Courage Ritual with Friends"; and "Spirit Succor: Spiritual Nurturing with Others."

Warnings aside, approach this trip as both a journey into nature and as a journey into yourself. Talk with your journey mates beforehand about how you can evoke the power of the wilderness to heal yourselves. You could work with your dreams, develop a healing ritual, meditate on a mountain or river, identify trees, do whatever will immerse you in the natural world. I find keeping my journal close by and writing about my experiences allows me to enter more deeply into the unfolding mystery. I also find it helps to have a beginning and ending ceremony of some kind. It could be as simple as joining hands and stating your intention for the retreat. What is important is to signal the beginning of the journey as a way to activate your unconscious and then acknowledge the end, thereby providing a sense of closure.

Trips for and by Women

See "Women for Comfort."

If arranging a trip on your own sounds overwhelming, consider attending one of the many trips to the wilderness led by women for women. Domestic or foreign, hard or easy, pick a trip that encompasses dreams: to white-water canoe, to climb a peak, to hike in Tibet, to kayak in the Sea of Cortez. Challenge and empower yourself! Wilderness trips can also be combined with other experiences: creative writing, Native American ritual, wilderness survival skills, herbal knowledge.

RESOURCES:

The Wild Within: Adventures in Nature and Animal Teachings, by Paul Rezendes (Berkeley Publishing Group, 1999). Thought-provoking book about tracking and how it can become a spiritual meditation.

The Spell of the Sensuous: Perception and Language in a More-Than-Human World, by David Abram (Vintage, 1997). A revolutionary look at where human and nonhuman intersect.

The Earth Speaks, by Steve Van Matre, illustrated by Gwen Frostic (Institute for Earth Education, 1985). A collection of images and impressions captured by those who have listened to the Earth with their hearts—John Muir, Walt Whitman, Annie Dillard, John Burroughs, Rachel Carson, Aldo Leopold, Henry David Thoreau, and more. Fantastic.

A *Nature Ritual*, by Selena Fox (Circle Sanctuary, 2002). Meditative affirmation. Available at http://www.circlesanctuary.org/aboutpagan/NatureRitual.html.

Yoga Vacations, by Annalisa Cunningham (John Muir Publications, 1999). Write-ups on international yoga retreats.

Yoga Escapes: A Yoga Journal Guide to the Best Places to Relax, Renew, and Reflect, by Jeanne Ricci (Celestial Arts, 2003). Another good guide.

Northwaters Wilderness Programs, Route 22, Westport, NY 12993. Phone (518) 962–4869 or visit http://www.northwaters.com or http://www. temagamivisionquest.com or http://www.texperience.com. Phenomenal programs for adults, children, and young adults. Located north of Toronto, Canada.

Cloud Canyon Expeditions, 4858 Ogram Road, Santa Barbara, CA 93105–9732. Visit http://www.cloudcanyon.com or phone (805) 692–9615. Women's backpacking pilgrimages in Utah backcountry. Experience the feminine red rock canyons led with love, safety, and inner challenge in mind.

SEASONAL COMFORTS

What Is It?

The wonders of living in the modern world are great. But getting out of touch with the Earth is one of the drawbacks. Paying attention to the rhythms of nature is a natural way to draw sustenance from life. We can reestablish our bond to the Earth and derive comfort and support from an almost inexhaustible source.

You'll Need:

Various seasonal accoutrements, like snowballs and watermelons, kites and tulips. Whatever is available and comforting.

When to Do It:

- When you've been locked in a hermetically sealed office building all week.
- When you can't remember the last time you did anything related to the natural rhythms of the seasons.
- When your present holiday rituals leave you empty and depressed.

What to Do:

Winter

Curl up in flannel sheets with someone you love, be they human or animal.

Design or buy a calendar for the new year.

Sip hot tea and watch the rain.

Make a snow angel.

Have a snowball fight, then run indoors and sip hot, mulled wine or apple cider by a roaring fire.

Roast marshmallows in the fireplace.

Make a steaming pot of soup or a hearty winter stew of root vegetables.

Bake bread.

Winter	*Summer*
Winter holidays	*Summer holidays*
Spring	*Fall*
Spring holidays	*Fall holidays*

Collect pinecones. Put them in an old pillow case, then dip in a gallon of water, mixed with a pound of either salt or borax. (Never mix the salt and borax together!) Spread the pinecones out to dry for several days. Burn them in your fireplace, and watch for their green and yellow flames.

Winter Holidays

Set aside an evening with close friends and family. Light a few candles, sip hot chocolate, and discuss what the holidays mean to each of you. Dig past the obvious.

Turn the pressure of corporate America off, and declare a no-shopping Christmas or Hanukkah. Practice the Native American tradition of give-aways during the holiday season by giving away useful or loved possessions instead of buying new.

Create new holiday rituals to replace painful or empty ones. You don't have to keep family traditions that don't make you feel good anymore. Try celebrating the winter solstice.

Do something you wish you had done as a child. Organize friends and put on a holiday play. Or have a potluck dinner for Thanksgiving with non-traditional foods. Consider serving foods you always wanted to eat as a child.

Spend some time on New Year's Eve thinking about your accomplishments in the past year. Praise yourself for everything you did, no matter how small.

Spring

Send a long-stemmed rose to someone you admire.

Walk around your neighborhood, and look for new growth: buds, bulbs, grass shoots.

Plant herbs in a pot of dirt on a windowsill.

Pin lilacs in your hair.

Investigate a mud puddle like a naturalist.

Plant daffodils, tulips, paper-white narcissi, and Easter lilies.

Plant a tree.

Climb a tree.

Visit garage sales or flea markets. Buy new patio or balcony furniture.

See "Heal Your Habitat."

Rearrange your furniture. Take up rugs, add plants, paint a ceiling the color of a robin's egg.

Have a tea party outdoors. Sip herbal tea and enjoy nature budding around you.

Visit a newborn baby.

Spring Holidays

Celebrate May Day (May 1). This festival comes to us from ancient tree-worshiping cults. Wear green and decorate a maypole with ribbons.

Throw a masked carnival, and celebrate new life by getting playful and zany.

Make a celebration out of opening the house up after the long winter. Call it a spring greening.

Celebrate the first day of spring by writing a current goal on a slip of paper and planting it with a single sunflower seed in a pot. Each time you water your seed, visualize your dream coming true, or plan the next step you will take. As your seedling grows into a plant, imagine your goal growing into fruition also. When the sunflower is finished blooming, scatter the seeds in nature. These scattered seeds represent the seeds for new dreams as well as the natural cycle of life.

Summer

Fill a plastic wading pool with water, and splash in it.

Go to the circus.

Have a sand-castle-building party.

Sing a serenade outdoors to someone you love.

Tie balloons to a friend's car.

Draw pictures on the sidewalk with colored chalk.

Eat ice cream while walking down a hot sidewalk. Let it drip all over your hands and face.

Make love under the stars.

Eat watermelon on a back porch. Spit the seeds as far as you can.

Watch a thunderstorm from someplace safe.

Make Popsicles.

Camp out in the backyard with your best friend. Tell ghost stories. Wake up at three and sneak back into your bed.

Go to a drive-in movie. Take a pizza.

Eat breakfast outside with the sun on your face.

Have a picnic on your lunch hour.

Summer Holidays

Celebrate the summer solstice. According to Z. Budapest, feminist witch, the summer solstice is a great time for wishing. Go to the nearest body of water with a flower, traditionally a rose, make a wish, kiss the flower, and let the water carry it away.

Fall

Run through a tall cornfield.

Let the wind push you down the sidewalk.

Fly a kite.

Go for a hayride.

Collect fall leaves. Even in Florida and southern California, you can find leaves that change. Make it a fall ritual to travel somewhere, even if it is only a few miles, to see the leaves changing.

Cook s'mores over an open fire.

Walk briskly, and sniff the fall air.

Pop corn.

Take a class in a subject you've always wanted to explore. Buy a crisp new notebook, yellow pencils, and kneesocks.

Howl at the moon.

Fall Holidays

Dress up for Halloween, and go trick-or-treating with children. Or put on a haunted house for adults only.

There are many timeworn legends attached to Halloween. Try celebrating this day by visiting the elderly or giving food to the poor.

RESOURCES:

Pilgrim at Tinker Creek, by Annie Dillard (Perennial, 1998). A book about seeing. See especially the chapter "Winter."

Earth Prayers, edited by Elizabeth Roberts and Elias Amidon (Harper-SanFrancisco, 1991). 365 prayers, poems, and invocations. Excellent for celebrating the passing of the seasons.

Home Comforts: The Art and Science of Keeping House, by Cheryl Mendelson, with illustrations by Harry Bates (Scribner, 1999). This is one of those books you either love and refer to often or despise and give to your anal retentive friend.

Four Seasons of Inner and Outer Beauty: Rituals and Recipes for Well-Being Throughout the Year, by Peggy Wynne Borgman (Broadway Books, 2000). Spa treatments, meditations, self-massage, botanical beauty treatments, aromatherapy, journal writing, and healing foods coordinated with the seasons.

Exploring the Labyrinth: A Guide for Healing and Spiritual Growth, by Melissa Gayle West (Broadway Books, 2000). What if you walked a labyrinth at the change of each season?

The Book of Ceremonies: A Native Way of Honoring and Living the Sacred, by Gabriel Horn, with illustrations by Carises Horn (New World Library, 2000). An eclectic Native collection of essays, songs, poems, prayers, and reflections on the cycles of the Earth and of human life.

The Healing Secrets of Food: A Practical Guide for Nourishing Body, Mind, and Soul, by Deborah Kesten (New World Library, 2001). Secrets include ways to eat with the seasons.

Website:

School of the Seasons
http://www.schooloftheseasons.com

HEAL YOUR HABITAT

What Is It?

We spend most of our lives indoors. In turn, we spend approximately eight to twelve hours a day at work, whether that be in our home or at an office, and another six to twelve hours in our bedrooms. Logically, these particular spaces should be as nurturing as possible. These rooms should help us do what we do in them better. Sadly, that is rarely the case. Whether office politics, small children, lack of time, or plain boredom is giving you the habitat blues, it's time to do something about it! You don't have to be rich or have an interior decorator to like where you work and live.

You'll Need:

Your senses.

Design books, decorating how-to books, home magazines.

When to Do It:

- When you find yourself not wanting to go home because it isn't a pleasant place.
- When you feel making your home comfortable is frivolous and a waste of time.
- When you feel trapped into living in an uncomfortable way.
- When your workplace depresses you instead of inspiring you.

What to Do:

Keep It Simple

We live in a world that encourages consumption. Consumption is not the key to comfort. Simplicity, on the other hand, may be, especially if you have little cash or are not handy around the house.

Keep it simple | *Office*
Decorate for your child within | *Transform your bedroom into a haven*
Bring nature inside | *A comfort kit*

A screenwriter and director I know lives in an apartment that embodies the Shaker style of simplicity. When you enter her home, you are struck by inviting emptiness: an expanse of wood floors, cane chairs around a small table, a few flowers in a vase.

Try getting rid of everything you own that you either:

a. hate to look at or

b. haven't used in a year.

Create out-of-sight storage for your needs. Walk around your house, and take note of what never has a place. In our house, it's shoes, papers, and tools. A basket in the kitchen can catch extra papers. A rack outside the back door can capture shoes. Wicker baskets peeking out from under your bed can store out-of-season clothes. You can use a screen to hide extra things. To make one, hinge together four artist's stretcher frames, pad the frames, and finish by stapling on sheets or fabric.

Filing cabinets can double as side tables, especially when hidden under tablecloths. Use them to organize all the paper that floods your life. File categories could include take-out menus, newspaper clippings, investment info, catalogs, and coupons.

Consider painting your rooms shades of one color, perhaps yellow or white. It is an easy way to pull a room together.

Decorate for Your Child Within

We are grown-ups now. (Or at least we're impersonating them.) We can decorate our houses and apartments any way we choose. An alternative to Shaker simplicity is colorful, jumbled, *fun*. To accomplish this, try painting your walls wild colors—raspberry, melon, leaf green. Experiment with different painting techniques. My husband used a rag to roll sea foam green on our dining room walls, then painted the plate rail in teal. The room can resemble either a Victorian greenhouse or a tropical paradise, depending on the tablecloth, plants, and objects displayed.

You can also paint furniture. Old chairs, dressers, and tables can be bought at yard sales and easily transformed into whimsical accents. Try combining several vibrant colors or using stencils.

Drape a soft fuzzy blanket, patchwork quilt, or cotton striped comforter over furniture. Fringed shawls, lace pillows, and flowered tablecloths can all express your playful side.

Cover the wall by your phone with butcher block paper, and doodle while talking.

Put things in unusual places: a hammock in the living room, an upholstered chair in the bath, a print hanging on a covered porch.

If part of you wants to decorate to comfort your child, and the other part loves another style, think about reserving one room for your inner child. A bedroom, study, and bath are good choices.

Bring Nature Inside

Put a hummingbird feeder outside your office or bedroom window.

See "Green Things" for info on forcing bulbs.

Add houseplants, especially fragrant flowering bulbs. You can use artificial lights for a windowless office. Bamboo, corkscrew willow, and Boston ferns add texture as well as greenery.

Fill a bowl with natural sponges, delicate river rocks, shells, or sea glass. Place the bowl where it will catch the afternoon light. Colored bottles on windowsills, prisms, and stained glass also help you notice the passing of another day.

Unusual fruits, vegetables, nuts, and flowers in a large bowl can make a seasonal and life-affirming centerpiece. Try frilly cabbages, fuzzy coconuts, dried chili peppers, intricate artichokes, glossy chestnuts, and a few daisies, and intertwine it all with ivy leaves.

Arrange dried rose hips, willow branches, New Zealand tea bush, or pod-shaped flowers in a tall vase near a window. Listen for their gentle rustle when the wind blows.

Consider hanging dried herbs from your kitchen ceiling or near your sink.

See "Herbal Help."

A scented geranium in a sunny bathroom may release its scent when you shower.

See "Sweet Scents: Scented Flowers and Plants."

Transform an ugly view by hanging a fern or a trailing ivy in front of the window.

Office

Can you paint your office? Creative ideas are thought to emerge best in a room with some red, while blue can reduce tension. A room painted the colors you like most can greatly enhance your performance.

See "Aesthetic Pleasures" for more ideas.

Have a piece of glass cut to fit your desktop. Stick favorite snapshots, art postcards, quotes, and other memorabilia underneath. Comforting glimpses will emerge from under your work all day. Change the items regularly.

Give some thought to how your office is arranged. Are you often frustrated by piles of paper, the phone in the wrong place, harsh afternoon sunlight on your computer screen? Spend a day noting what the layout problems are. Do you need better task lighting; accessories to hold papers, clips, and pens; more desk space? Take the time to improve whatever you can.

Transform Your Bedroom into a Haven

This is an especially good idea if you have small children or roommates. Your bedroom can be the only room off-limits to everyone else.

If you share this room with a partner, sit down and discuss how to change the room. Talk about your different needs and tastes.

Try painting the walls using a marine sponge to apply a coat of violet, then a coat of sky blue, and then a coat of white. The effect is cloudy and soothing.

Paint your ceiling powder or sky blue.

Buy blackout blinds for your windows, or wear a sleeping mask.

See "A Personal Sanctuary."

Create a personal sanctuary in one corner.

Make your bed the most cushy, warm, sensual nest you can. Place a feather bed or extra fluffy cotton comforter on top of your mattress. Add lots of pillows, soft cotton sheets, a silk shawl. Think tactile comfort.

Bring music into your bedroom.

Place a fluffy rug next to your bed.

Give yourself a view first thing in the morning: a framed print, a vase of fresh flowers, a blooming violet, a lace panel, or a Chinese paper screen over a window.

Arrange votive candles on a metal tray in place of a fire.

A Comfort Kit

A comfort kit is a bag of goodies to carry with you. You might include a small teddy bear or other comforting creatures, healthy snacks you selected when you weren't depressed or stressed, phone numbers of friends you can call if you get down, a sweet scent that reminds you of good times, a picture of a happy event, perhaps your comfort journal and some crayons. When Paula Steinmetz, a therapist in west Los Angeles, recommends comfort kits to her clients, she suggests carrying your sponsor's telephone number and a list of meetings if you are working a twelve-step program, exercise clothes and jogging shoes, and index cards with current affirmations.

You can change and mold this comfort kit for different occasions and moods. You might have a small bag you carry with work comforts inside, and a larger bag you take to your parents' or lover's house for the week-end.

Carry your comfort kit on rainy days, when you travel, when you're having a bad day, to your workplace if it is a cold or stressful place, any time the reassurance will ease your path.

See "A Personal Sanctuary: A Comfort Box" for a variation.

RESOURCES:

Paint Magic, by Jocasta Innes (Frances Lincoln, 2004). Painting techniques including sponging and furniture painting.

Shelter for the Spirit: Create Your Own Haven in a Hectic World, by Victoria Moran (Perennial, 1998). One of the first and best books to address creating a sense of peace and renewal in your home.

Simple Pleasures of the Home: Cozy Comforts and Old-Fashioned Crafts for Every Room in the House, by Susannah Seton (Conari, 1999). Non–Martha Stewart ideas for creating comfort.

Home Sanctuary: Practical Ways to Create a Spiritually Fulfilling Environment, by Nicole Marcelis (McGraw-Hill, 2000). Draws on many techniques—feng shui, color therapy, aromatherapy, space clearing, symbolism—to help you create a home that is spiritually restful.

Holistic Home: Creating an Environment for Physical and Spiritual Well-Being, by Joanna Trevelyan (Sterling, 1998). A visual and informative treasure trove.

Open House: Writers Redefine Home—Graywolf Forum Five, edited by Mark Doty (Graywolf Press, 2003). Nineteen edgy, unexpected outlooks on the question, "Where do you live?"

COMFORT CLOTHING

What Is It?

Consider the extraordinary amount of attention given to women's dress. Is it any wonder most of us are confused and uncomfortable about clothing ourselves? What would happen if we dressed to feel good, to reflect our inner spirit, and forgot about projecting an image, looking thin, or wearing the right colors?

You'll Need:

A large piece of poster board, fashion magazines, catalogs, scissors, and glue.

Your closet.

Your journal.

When to Do It:

- When you find yourself saying, "When I lose ten pounds, then I will buy something I love."
- When you find yourself not going to parties or other events because you've got nothing to wear.
- When you feel you can't afford new clothes, but when you desperately need something to wear, you run out and guiltily buy something that you then hate and never wear.

What to Do:

Clothing Visualization

Put your poster board, fashion magazines, scissors, and glue on a nearby work surface.

Relax. Close your eyes. Picture yourself in an everyday scene wearing clothing that makes you feel confident, comfortable, secure. Forget what you usually wear or what you think you should wear. Concentrate on visualizing yourself in the most comforting clothing you can imagine. Notice the details of your comfort clothing. What does the fabric feel like? What kind of shoes do you have on? What colors have you chosen?

Now imagine yourself wearing another comforting outfit in a different situation, for example, envision yourself at work, wearing clothes that make you feel great. Now, allow your inner eye to wander through a few more settings. See yourself playing with friends, at a party, doing errands. In each situation, you are wearing truly comforting clothes. When you are ready, take a long, slow breath, open your eyes, and begin leafing through fashion magazines and catalogs. Whenever you see an image that grabs you—that relates to your visualization—cut it out.

Pile your images near your poster board. You are going to construct a collage of a comfort style that both expresses your visualization and also reflects what you will look good in. This is possible! The key is to concentrate on the total picture. Move images around, play with shapes and colors, while keeping in the back of your mind your lifestyle and body type. If you find an image you are in love with, but you can't imagine wearing it, glue it on the back. You can also draw, sketch, or write observations, anything that will give form to your new comfort image. Take all the time you need to construct your collage.

Comfort Closet

Prop your collage nearby to use as a divining tool. Try on your very favorite outfit. Admire yourself in it. Then hang it in your closet. From now on, only clothing that expresses the inner you, makes you feel terrific, and fits is allowed inside your closet. Continue trying on or examining all your clothes. If you are not absolutely thrilled by something you try on, put it in the discard pile. Do not start a maybe pile or a when-I-get-thin pile! If you are in doubt, glance at your collage. Does it fit in? If not, chuck it.

If you keep all your "mistakes" (all the clothes you will someday fit in, all the classics that went out of date five years ago) every time you open your closet door you will feel bad. Ugly. Guilty. If you are terribly attached to some items or feel extravagant throwing them away, store them elsewhere: under the bed, in the hall closet, even in the garage (in a garment bag). Try to remove everything from your closet that is not comfortable, in both the physical and emotional sense of the word. It will make clothing yourself a completely different experience.

Time-Is-Life Clothing List

Make a list of all the activities for which you feel you have nothing comfortable to wear. Examples might include hanging out with friends, running errands, or entertaining clients at home.

Sit down with this list and your collage. Make a list of what you need to fill in your gaps. Study your collage for ideas. Take several days or even weeks to create this new list. If you need more ideas, window-shop, look at more catalogs and magazines, or ask a trusted friend with great style to give you an opinion.

Shopping

Before you say you can't afford anything new, consider this: if you continue to shop according to frustration, panic, and disappointment, you will continue to fill your closets with uncomfortable clothes that make you feel bad. And that is something you really can't afford.

Plan, plan, and plan before you shop. Don't wait until the last minute before you need something. Decide what shops you will visit, and exactly what items you will be looking for. Don't look for too many things at a time. When you start to get tired, find a comfortable, quiet corner to sip something cool and to visualize the outfit you are looking for. When you get tired, *leave*. Bad purchases are often made at the end of the shopping day!

RESOURCES:

Secrets of a Fashion Therapist: What You Can Learn Behind the Dressing Room Door, by Betty Halbreich (Cliff Street Books, 2000). Become a well-dressed, savvy shopper without buying into the beauty myth.

Does This Make Me Look Fat? The Definitive Rules for Dressing Thin for Every Height, Size, and Shape, by Leah Feldon (Villard, 2002). Lots and lots of real life information.

Forty Over Forty: Forty Things Every Woman over Forty Needs to Know About Getting Dressed, by Brenda Reiten Kinsel and Jenny M. Phillips (Wildcat Canyon Press, 2000). Excellent guide for forty and older—spend less time and money!

NURTURE YOUR BODY IMAGE

What Is It?

I can think of only three women I know who are at peace with their physical being. Even my thin and beautiful friends complain about their hips or their noses or even their feet!

The majority of us are locked into a painful distortion of our body images. We are caught between society's image of beauty and our own image in the mirror. Society has set impossible standards that have left almost every woman wanting to change something about herself. This can't be right!

You cannot nourish yourself if you hate the body you live in. Enjoying and accepting your body is a fundamental aspect of nurturing and accepting yourself as a woman. The exercises below are offered as a loving balm to your wounded body image. Try them, and see if you don't feel more comfortable in the envelope of your skin.

You'll Need:

A full-length mirror.

Your comfort journal and a pen.

When to Do It:

- When you find yourself saying, "I will try _________ when I lose ___ pounds."
- When you are haunted by parental or other voices saying, "You're too chubby" or "tall" or "lumpy" or "hairy."
- When you look in the mirror and loathe your body.

What to Do:

Moving Affirmations

This exercise is based in part on an exercise found in Marcia Hutchinson's book *Transforming Body Image*.

Moving affirmations   *Give your body a break*
Mirror affirmations

Create affirmations that describe how you would like to feel about your body. Always phrase them in the present tense, as if they were already true.

Examples are:

I like my body and feel totally comfortable in it now.

See "Ease into Comforting Yourself."

I am perfectly all right the way I am.

I am strong and supple.

Every cell in my body is bursting with beauty and health.

Now, while repeating your affirmation aloud or to yourself, express your affirmation in movement. Walk the way you would walk if your affirmation were true. Breathe it in, dance it out, exude it to the world. If this feels too weird, try repeating your body affirmations while walking, biking, swimming, having sex, or doing any kind of movement you enjoy.

Mirror Affirmations

Look at yourself in a mirror, and repeat *aloud* one body affirmation. Vary it. For example:

I, Jennifer Louden, now love my healthy body.

I love my healthy body.

Jennifer Louden loves her healthy body.

Give Your Body a Break

Stand naked in front of a full-length mirror. (Don't panic! I know this can be difficult. Please, just try.)

Close your eyes, and breathe deeply for a few moments.

Open your eyes. Study your body, front and back, for a full minute. Try not to react, just observe.

Now, take a deep breath, and focus on a part of your body you love. Admire this favorite feature of yours. Experience as completely as possible your pleasure and pride in this part of your body. Bring your nurturing voice in to help you express your love.

NURTURE YOUR BODY IMAGE

See "Your Nurturing Voice."

Close your eyes. Continue to feel good feelings about your loved feature. Open your eyes and focus on a part of your body you dislike. Let the good feelings for your loved feature flow over onto the disliked feature. It may feel strange, but keep going. It helps to glance back at the body part you like.

Every other day, work with another body part. Keep going back to the stubborn ones.

End this by gently caressing your newly loved body parts, or try one of the self-touch exercises in the "Touch" chapter.

RESOURCES:

Bodylove, by Rita Freedman, Ph.D. (Gurze Books, 2002). Love your physical self.

Fit from Within, by Victoria Moran (McGraw-Hill, 2003). Using self-acceptance, self-nurturing, and spirituality, learn the "simple secrets" Moran used to lose sixty pounds for good.

200 Ways to Love the Body You Have, by Marcia Germaine Hutchinson (Crossing Press, 1999). Accessible ways to inhabit your body and leave self-hatred behind.

The Power of Focusing: A Practical Guide to Emotional Self-Healing, by Ann Weiser Cornell (New Harbinger, 1996). A powerful, fast, body-centered way to know what you really think and feel.

Jumpstart Your Metabolism: How to Lose Weight by Changing the Way You Breathe, by Pam Grout (Fireside, 1998). My point in including this book is not to focus you on losing weight but on experiencing the possibilities of the breath.

Comfort at a Glance

	INTRODUCTION	ABOUT RELAXING	CHECKING YOUR BASIC NEEDS	COMFORT JOURNAL	A SELF-CARE SCHEDULE	EASE INTO COMFORTING YOURSELF	YOUR NURTURING VOICE	CREATIVE SELFISHNESS	COMFORT RITUALS	A PERSONAL SANCTUARY	CREATING A COMFORT NETWORK	COURAGE RITUALS	MONEY, MONEY, MONEY	COMFORTING COMMUNICATION	WOMEN FOR COMFORT	COMFORT CARDS	A DAY OFF	HIDING UNDER THE COVERS	BECOMING A GURU OF PLAY	READING AS A CHILD	GET SILLY	ANIMAL ANTIDOTES	GREEN THINGS	NATURE'S SOLACE	SEASONAL COMFORTS	HEAL YOUR HABITAT
Afraid to Be Alone						22	24				43	48														
Aging			6				24																	95	99	105
Angry								28						58												
Anxious		5			16	20	24		33	39						65		72						94		
Arguments											44			58		65					82					
Bored				9	18	20				39		49					68		76	79	81		89		98	
Broke							24				43	50	53													104
Burned-Out	1		6		14	20		28		39															98	
Can't Find the Money for Fun											43		53													104
Can't Find Time to Nurture Yourself			6		14	20	24	28		39				58			68	72								108
Can't Hear Your Intuition			6				24						53													
Can't Say No			6					30				49		58												
Can't Sleep				11					33				53													107
Confused														58			68	72			81					
Controlling		5				20	24										68	72	76	79	81	86	91	93		
Cramps																							91			
Crowded								30		39							68							95		107
Cynical																			76	79			89	93	98	
Denial						20	24					50														
Depressed			6	12		22	24		33	39	43		54	58	62	65		72				86				
Deprived			6	11	18			28					53				68									105
Disconnected	2			9		22	24		37		43			58	61							85	89	94	98	
Disorganized		5			16			28																		105
Disappointed							24		37						61	65		72								
Distrustful											45			58	61							85				
Don't Know How to Start Caring for Yourself	1	5				20											68		76						98	
Embarrassment							24					49				65		72			82					

Comfort at a Glance

COMFORT CLOTHING	NURTURE YOUR BODY IMAGE	WHEN I THINK OF COMFORT, I THINK OF FOOD	TOUCH	SELF-PLEASURING	BODY DELIGHTS	BATHING PLEASURES	SWEET SCENTS	HERBAL HELP	AESTHETIC PLEASURES	QUIET, PLEASE	SOOTHING SOUNDS	NUTRITIONAL MUSIC	SPIRIT SUCCOR	SOLITUDE	LITTLE LOSSES	LETTING OFF STEAM	A FORGIVENESS RITUAL	THE SHADOW SIDE OF COMFORT	CHALLENGE COMFORT	THE POWER OF GOALS	NURTURE OTHERS	SIMPLIFY	REMINDING YOURSELF	A FEW LAST THINGS	
													166	173	175										Afraid to be Alone
110	113												169	172											Aging
												164				178	182								Angry
		126	129		137					157	159			173								203			Anxious
			131								159					178	182				200				Arguments
			128	132	136				153				169						190	194	200				Bored
															175	178				194					Broke
			129		137	145		150	154			163	166		175								205		Burned-Out
110																		186		194	200	203			Can't Find the Money for Fun
												163		172								203			Can't Find Time to Nurture Yourself
		123												172				185				203			Can't Hear Your Intuition
										157				172						194					Can't Say No
			129	132					155	157	159	163	166				182								Can't Sleep
										157				172					192				205		Confused
				132					155												199				Controlling
			129	132	137	145		151																	Cramps
													166	172		178									Crowded
									153				167				182	184	190	197	199				Cynical
														172	175			184							Denial
	113	123	131		136		143	149			159	164	166		175	178					199	203	205		Depressed
110			128						153				166		175					194					Deprived
									153		159					180					200				Disconnected
110																						203			Disorganized
															175	178	182		192						Disappointed
													168				182				199				Distrustful
112	114	122			136								169							194		203		208	Don't Know How to Start Caring for Yourself
110															175	180	182		192		200				Embarrassment

Comfort at a Glance

	INTRODUCTION	ABOUT RELAXING	CHECKING YOUR BASIC NEEDS	COMFORT JOURNAL	A SELF-CARE SCHEDULE	EASE INTO COMFORTING YOURSELF	YOUR NURTURING VOICE	CREATIVE SELFISHNESS	COMFORT RITUALS	A PERSONAL SANCTUARY	CREATING A COMFORT NETWORK	COURAGE RITUALS	MONEY, MONEY, MONEY	COMFORTING COMMUNICATION	WOMEN FOR COMFORT	COMFORT CARDS	A DAY OFF	HIDING UNDER THE COVERS	BECOMING A GURU OF PLAY	READING AS A CHILD	GET SILLY	ANIMAL ANTIDOTES	GREEN THINGS	NATURE'S SOLACE	SEASONAL COMFORTS	HEAL YOUR HABITAT
Emptiness				9																		85	89	93	98	
Exhausted	1	5	6		20			28	33									72	76							
Failure												49				65										108
Feeling Fat and Ugly												49														
Frazzled	1	5	6			20												72	76	79	81		91		98	
Frustrated								30						58				73			81					104
Grief							24				45			58		65										
Guilty						21		29					56					73								
Had an Awful Day	1		6		14	20		31						58	62	65				79	83	86			98	107
Help Planning Self-Care		5		10	14	20	24	30									68									
Hopeless							24									65						85	89	93	100	
Ignored																										
Ill	2		6		18	22	24		35							65	68	72								107
Inadequate							24							58	61	65		72			83					
Incompetent							24					48				65					83					
Injured	3						24									65		72		79		86				
Insecurity						21	24		34	39			53	58	61	65						85				
Isolation			6	12							43			58	61							85	89	93		106
Joyless			6		18		24						53				69		76	79	81	85	89	93	98	
Lonely						22	24				43			58	62		70		76			86	89	95		108
Lover/Mate Trouble								29	34			48	56	58							82					108
Lustful										39																
Moving			6				24		35	39		50													100	108
Need a Pick-Me-Up				12		20						50				65				79	81		89	95	98	106
Needy			6					28		39				58								85				108
Nervous			6									49		58								85				
Nothing to Wear							24																			
Old							24		36			48		58	61	65			76	79	81			95	98	
Out of Touch with Nature																			76			86	89	93	98	106

Comfort at a Glance

COMFORT CLOTHING	NURTURE YOUR BODY IMAGE	WHEN I THINK OF COMFORT, I THINK OF FOOD	TOUCH	SELF-PLEASURING	BODY DELIGHTS	BATHING PLEASURES	SWEET SCENTS	HERBAL HELP	AESTHETIC PLEASURES	QUIET, PLEASE	SOOTHING SOUNDS	NUTRITIONAL MUSIC	SPIRIT SUCCOR	SOLITUDE	LITTLE LOSSES	LETTING OFF STEAM	A FORGIVENESS RITUAL	THE SHADOW SIDE OF COMFORT	CHALLENGE COMFORT	THE POWER OF GOALS	NURTURE OTHERS	SIMPLIFY	REMINDING YOURSELF	A FEW LAST THINGS	
									153				166	173	175						199				Emptiness
						140		149		157											203	205	207		Exhausted
											159				175				192	196					Failure
110	113	122	129		136	140	145	149				163			175										Feeling Fat and Ugly
						140	145	149	154	157	159	163	166	172								203			Frazzled
					137											178						203			Frustrated
													166		175		182				199				Grief
		122															182	186		197					Guilty
		122	129	132	137	140	145	149			159	163	166	172	175	178	182	185						207	Had an Awful Day
112														173				186		194			205	207	Help Planning Self-Care
			128			142			154			164	166		175		182	187			199				Hopeless
			128									164	168								200				Ignored
	113		128		137	140	145	149				163													Ill
	113												168		175					194			205		Inadequate
					138				155		159				175				192	194					Incompetent
	113		128			140	145	149				163					182								Injured
	113												166						191				205		Insecurity
											159		168	173				188	190						Isolation
			128	132	138				153			163	166	172	175					196			205		Joyless
	113		128	132								163						188	190		199				Lonely
				132		142								172	175	178									Lover/Mate Trouble
			128	132	137	140																			Lustful
									153				170							194	199				Moving
		126	128	132	136	141	146	151	154	157	159	163		172											Need a Pick-Me-Up
					137								166	173											Needy
		122				141	145	149		157	159	163							191						Nervous
110	113																					203			Nothing to Wear
110	113		128	132	136										175					194			205		Old
							143	149					168							193					Out of Touch with Nature

Comfort at a Glance

	INTRODUCTION	ABOUT RELAXING	CHECKING YOUR BASIC NEEDS	COMFORT JOURNAL	A SELF-CARE SCHEDULE	EASE INTO COMFORTING YOURSELF	YOUR NURTURING VOICE	CREATIVE SELFISHNESS	COMFORT RITUALS	A PERSONAL SANCTUARY	CREATING A COMFORT NETWORK	COURAGE RITUALS	MONEY, MONEY, MONEY	COMFORTING COMMUNICATION	WOMEN FOR COMFORT	COMFORT CARDS	A DAY OFF	HIDING UNDER THE COVERS	BECOMING A GURU OF PLAY	READING AS A CHILD	GET SILLY	ANIMAL ANTIDOTES	GREEN THINGS	NATURE'S SOLACE	SEASONAL COMFORTS	HEAL YOUR HABITAT
Over-Committed		5	6		14	20	24	30	36	39							68	72			81				98	
Over-Eating																										
Over-Whelmed		5				20	24	30	33	39	43						68	72	76		81					108
Over-Worked																		72								107
PMS		5								39								72							98	
Powerless			6				24					48														
Pressured	1	5	6		14	20	24	28						58	61	65	68	72	76		81				98	108
Procrastinating					14								55													
Regrets							24									65						85			99	
Rejected						20	24	28			43				61			72				85	89			
Resentful			6										53	58												
Restless				12	14												69		76	79	82	85	89	96	98	104
Rushed		5	6		14	20	24	30						58											98	
Sad									37					58		65		72				85	89	93		
Scared							24					48	53	58												
Self-Loathing						21	24		36			48														
Shame			6				24					48														
Spiritually Bankrupt				9							43				62									93		
Stifled Creativity				9					34						61	65			76	79	81		89		98	105
Stinky																							91			
Stuck in a Rut			6	11					34		43						70	72		79	81				100	
Temper Tantrum			6											58												
Tense		5		12		20	24			39							68	72	76		81	86		93	98	
Too Serious	1	5		11		20	24										68	72	76	79	81	85				
Trapped			6					28			43		53													
Traveling							24			39		48	53			65	68				82		92	96		108
Uncomfortable			6						33																	104
Unconscious			6		14								55													
Uninspired				9													68		76	79	83		89	93	98	
Vices							24					48	53													

Comfort at a Glance

COMFORT CLOTHING	NURTURE YOUR BODY IMAGE	WHEN I THINK OF COMFORT, I THINK OF FOOD	TOUCH	SELF-PLEASURING	BODY DELIGHTS	BATHING PLEASURES	SWEET SCENTS	HERBAL HELP	AESTHETIC PLEASURES	QUIET, PLEASE	SOOTHING SOUNDS	NUTRITIONAL MUSIC	SPIRIT SUCCOR	SOLITUDE	LITTLE LOSSES	LETTING OFF STEAM	A FORGIVENESS RITUAL	THE SHADOW SIDE OF COMFORT	CHALLENGE COMFORT	THE POWER OF GOALS	NURTURE OTHERS	SIMPLIFY	REMINDING YOURSELF	A FEW LAST THINGS	
						142		149			159					178	182			194		203	205	207	Over-Committed
110	113	122	128		136										175								205		Over-Eating
						142	143	149	154	157			166	173		178		187		194		203			Over-Whelmed
														172											Over-Worked
		122	129			142		149				163													PMS
													169					184	190	194			205		Powerless
									154			163		173		178						203			Pressured
																		187		194		203			Procrastinating
	113												166	172	175		182								Regrets
	114											163			175	178	182		192	194					Rejected
											159					178	182			196					Resentful
		122	128	132	136				155		159		166	173		178			190						Restless
		126																				203			Rushed
		126	131									164	167	173	175										Sad
																			191						Scared
	113	125	129	132		142							166		175								205		Self-Loathing
	113	125				142									175		182								Shame
									153				166	172			182				199				Spiritually Bankrupt
110									154		159		169	173					190	197					Stifled Creativity
							143	149																	Stinky
110				132	136				153		159		169		175				190	194	199	203			Stuck in a Rut
					137						159					178	182								Temper Tantrum
			129	132	137	140	143	149	154	157		164	166	172	175								205	207	Tense
		126							153				169							197			205		Too Serious
																178			190	194		203			Trapped
110			128								159	164													Traveling
110	113																	184	190						Uncomfortable
			128			142							166	173				185		194					Unconscious
			128						153			163	169	173					190	194				207	Uninspired
		122																184							Vices

WHEN I THINK OF COMFORT, I THINK OF FOOD

What Is It?

I think of brownies, coffee cake, mashed potatoes, macaroni and cheese, tuna noodle casserole, grilled cheese sandwiches, and chocolate chip cookies. Comfort foods are childlike, familiar, usually fattening, the stuff we automatically reach for when we are depressed. Food can be instant solace for our hurting hearts or our disappointed souls.

Food and women are inextricably wound together. Food is nurturance and comfort. Food is also body weight and body image. Food is a powerful and often ritualistic way to nurture the people we love. But if we overeat, we are indulging, being greedy and needy, which is unacceptable. How are we supposed to have a healthy relationship with food? How can we use food as comfort, without it being a dangerous anesthetic?

You'll Need:

Food you love.

Courage.

When to Do It:

- When you are miserable about how you presently use food to comfort yourself.
- When you feel guilty every time you eat.
- If the above list of food made your palms sweat.

What to Do:

Truly Comfort Yourself

You've just had an awful day. Your car broke down, your cat got sick, your partner forgot your birthday. . . . You run home, reaching for the half gallon of rocky road ice cream, the leftover Thai noodles, and the cherry pie as soon as you can get in the door.

Stop. Sit down. Anywhere. Tell yourself you will only pause for two or three minutes. When you are finished, you can eat whatever you want. Really. No guilt, no restrictions.

Close your eyes. Breathe in and out five times. Gently ask yourself, "Why do I want to eat?" To feel better, because you are lonely, because you are disappointed or hurt, because life stinks? Know *why* you are eating. It might occur to you that taking care of yourself in some other way would make you feel better. Getting angry at your partner, taking a walk, or buying a new sweater might help. If so, go do one of those things now. Or you may still feel eating is what will help. Fine. Take one more minute to ask yourself, "What specific food do I want?" Forget what is in the refrigerator, what you planned for dinner, what you usually eat when you are in this mood. Just for a minute, imagine anything is available to you. What kind of taste, temperature, texture do you crave? If you can decide on a food, give it to yourself. If your guilty "I shouldn't be doing this" voice pipes up, shut her up with your nurturing voice. While you are eating, allow your nurturing voice to speak, telling you how good it is that you are taking care of yourself, that eating is just one more way to take good care of yourself.

See "Checking Your Basic Needs: A Good Question" and "The Shadow Side of Comfort: Mindful Comfort."

See "Your Nurturing Voice."

The bottom line is if you eat what you truly want, you'll end up eating less and you will be genuinely comforted. If you eat a ham sandwich because it's dinnertime but you really wanted a cup of creamy cappuccino and a buttery croissant from the bakery down the street, you will end up not feeling comforted by the food and possibly even driving to the bakery later and eating ten croissants! (Okay, maybe not ten. . . .)

Trust yourself enough to learn if food is sincerely what you need and, if so, what food. The little time it takes can turn an uncomfortable, self-negating experience into warm and deeply nurturing self-care.

Long-Term Comfort with Food

To achieve a healthy balance and positive nurturing relationship with food over the long haul, yet still comfort yourself, you need to do only two things:

1. Eat whatever you crave.

2. Eat only when you are hungry.

No food is banned. Strike the words *bad, fattening, caloric,* and *forbidden* from your vocabulary. Rediscover what it means to be hungry and what it feels like to give yourself exactly what you want.

Do you imagine yourself going wild, consuming the world, never being able to stop? Can you remember or imagine a world without diets or restrictions or guilt?

We eat for so many reasons, very few of which have anything to do with nourishing our bodies. If we can learn to trust ourselves long enough to feel hungry, but not starving, we can establish an honestly nurturing relationship with food. It won't happen overnight, but it will work. We won't eat the entire cookie section of the supermarket, we won't chew off our arms, and we won't end up weighing four hundred pounds.

Here are a few ways to approach eating what you want:

Don't be afraid to be hungry. The physical sensation of being hungry is natural and strangely pleasant, like a sore muscle after a day of playing. Physical hunger is not emotional hunger.

To eat what you honestly want means being able to change your mind, even if you have just cooked a full turkey dinner and suddenly discover that all you want is a chocolate eclair. This part drives a lot of people crazy. We've been told never to waste food. While I agree it is good not to waste food, you are learning here and so you get to make some new rules. Don't be afraid to change your mind at the last minute. If you are in a restaurant, ask to change your order, try to switch with a friend, take it home in a doggie bag, freeze it, or even throw it away. If you are at home, wrap it up and either prepare or go out and buy what you are honestly hungry for. It can be difficult, but the rewards are great.

Skip your regular mealtimes for a few days. Carry food with you so you will not be anxious if you are stranded someplace where food is not readily available.

Bingeing

When we eat a handful of chocolate chip cookies followed by a bowl of ice cream, a hot dog, and then french fries, we are sending a very strong signal to ourselves: *We need care*.

When we binge in any way, shape, or form, we are sending a clear signal to ourselves that we need more attention, not less. Unfortunately, because we feel terribly guilty after devouring a lot of food, we crack down on ourselves with diets, self-punishing exercise, wearing tight and uncomfortable clothing, and keeping up a constant barrage of self-hate in our brains. Please don't do this to yourself!

Whether bingeing for you is two chocolate chip cookies or all the cookies you can carry, please try to summon the courage to care for yourself right now instead of hating yourself.

Geneen Roth, author of *Breaking Free from Compulsive Eating*, believes we stuff our faces instead of watching soap operas or reading romance novels or lying in a hammock because it is more culturally acceptable for women to eat ourselves into oblivion than to just do nothing. I agree. Our society places a high premium on achievement. Achievement comes from doing. Eating qualifies as doing, but lying in a hammock does not.

Thwart this insidious belief. Allow yourself one thing a day that is frivolous and socially unacceptable but that nurtures you. One of my choices is reading home magazines. Can you allow yourself an equally frivolous, just for you, daily pleasure, especially after bingeing?

See "Ease into Comforting Yourself" for starter ideas.

Also, consider if you are eating to replace contact. Try reaching out to a friend or lover instead of or before you eat. Try picking up the phone, going over to your neighbor's, surprising your partner by picking him or her up from work. Move yourself into the flow of people; touch, speak, laugh.

Comfort Food Ritual for the Child Within

When we eat comfort food, we may be trying to comfort the part of us that is still a child. When we put restrictions on foods, decide to diet, or eat when we're not hungry, we are hurting this inner child. Soothe this part of yourself next time you are hurting by nurturing your child within.

Any time you ask yourself, "Why do I want to eat?" and the reason is at all related to childhood memories, feelings of abandonment, or not being taken care of, do this simple ritual.

Spend a few minutes imagining what food would comfort your child self. Close your eyes, and let your imagination roam. Imagine there are no restrictions, no diets, no five food groups. You can eat whatever the small child inside you craves. When you discover what you want, go get it. If it is not readily available, call a friend to bring it over or make the effort to get it. *Don't settle for less than what you really want.* (I keep saying this, but I found it to be the key to genuinely comforting myself with food.)

Eat your child-in-you comfort food out of fun dishes. A bowl decorated with Peter Rabbit? An oversized silver spoon? A bib? Eat someplace comforting, too. Under the covers with a teddy bear? Curled up on the couch with a blanket? While you are eating, pat your stomach and talk kindly to your child within. Hug a stuffed animal or beloved pet. Make smacking noises. Play with your food. Let yourself be and eat like a child, and see if you don't feel totally comforted.

Food Transition Ritual

The time between work and home life, before or after a date, or when we are switching between one time of the day and the next are times of transition. During these times I tend to turn to food for solace, and yet food usually is not what I really want.

If you find yourself stuck in transition times and not sure what to do with yourself but eat, and you're not hungry and would rather care for yourself in another manner, try inventing a small ritual instead. After work, you might take a quick shower or sing along with Bonnie Raitt for fifteen minutes. While waiting for a friend, you could water your plants. I like to straighten the house and then read a magazine or spend a few minutes out back, poking in my flower garden, or lie in my hammock in the sun and be still. By consciously choosing one or two things ahead of time, I can slip easily into these rituals, and they become familiar friends, comforting customs for those awkward moments and offering the same feeling as a glass of wine or fifty Doritos. There are times when only the glass of wine will do. But this way, I am giving myself options!

RESOURCES:

Much of this chapter is based on the brilliant work of Geneen Roth and Susie Orbach, both experts in women's relationship to food.

Feeding the Hungry Heart (Plume, 1993), *Why Weight?* (Plume, 1993), *When Food Is Love* (Plume, 1993), and *When You Eat at the Refrigerator, Pull Up a Chair* (Hyperion, 1999), all by Geneen Roth. Read these and never diet again.

The Hungry Self, by Kim Chernin (Perennial, 1994). An exploration of women's identities and how they relate to eating disorders.

Appetites: Why Women Want, by Caroline Knapp (Counterpoint Press, 2003). A fierce memoir of Knapp's battle with anorexia and an exploration of women's repressed desires. Wonderful.

It's Not About Food: Change Your Mind; Change Your Life; End Your Obsession with Food and Weight, by Carol Emery Normandi and Laurelee Roark (Penguin, 1999). Free yourself from "diet mentality."

Eating in the Light of the Moon: How Women Can Transform Their Relationship With Food Through Myths, Metaphors, and Storytelling, by Anita A. Johnston, Ph.D. (Gurze Books, 2000). Discover the metaphors hidden in your life stories.

TOUCH

What Is It?

Touch is our most important sense. Without it we would die. Yet we often neglect this vital source of comfort. We get medical checkups and make sure we eat well, but we pay little attention to our need to be touched and to touch others.

You can change that. Every square inch of your fingers has thirteen hundred nerve endings. This means there are hundreds of thousands of delicious, subtle, and healthy ways to comfort yourself. You can remedy the frustrations of life, both physical and mental, by regularly making time for touch and sensory exploration in your life.

You'll Need:

Your hands.

Massage oil.

Nature.

A friend's hands.

When to Do It:

- When you are under a lot of stress.
- When you are spending too much time alone.
- When you yearn to feel more intimately connected with life.

What to Do:

Touch Walk

Explore nature with your fingers, hands, cheeks, feet. You can do this alone or with a friend, taking turns blindfolding and guiding each other. A garden is bursting with unbelievable textures and feelings. Tickle yourself with the feathery lightness of a fern. Rub a smooth river rock against your palm. Caress a furry geranium leaf. Walk across the scratchy warmth of a concrete patio. Hold a struggling fish.

A Self-Massage

You can start this exercise with a warm bath.

Rub your hands together rapidly until they feel warm. Place your hands on your face. Hold them for a few seconds. Place two fingers from each hand in the center of your forehead. Rub in a circular motion toward and around your temples. Slide the heels of your palms to the tops of your cheekbones. Rub them in a circular motion downward over your cheeks, out toward your ears, and over your jaw bones.

Move your hands to your head. Place your fingers near the back of your head and your thumbs behind your ears. Bring your thumbs and fingers together. Move slowly forward and then back, massaging your scalp. Gently grasp your hair and move the skin of the scalp in different directions. Tap your fingers vigorously over your scalp. Now bring your fingers down to the middle of the back of your neck. Rub in a circular motion.

You could end the massage here with a facial treatment.

Or keep going by placing your right hand on your left shoulder. Stretch your head gently to the right. With your fingers together, firmly run them up your neck muscles, to your ear. Switch and repeat.

Slide your hands to your arms and knead, as if you were making bread. Always work toward your heart.

Take a moment to study your hand. Lightly follow the vein structure. Pull each finger, twisting slightly. Squeeze and pull the fleshly part between your thumb and first finger. Push your knuckles into the palm. Don't forget the other hand.

Rub your back with a back brush, sponge, or back scratcher. Try lying on the floor and rolling your back over a ball. Different sizes reach different muscles. Experiment with a small child's ball, a tetherball, and a volleyball. See which feels best.

Massage your lower back by placing your thumbs in the small of your back. Move your thumbs and fingers together, grabbing and kneading the flesh.

Lie on your side and make a fist. Push your knuckles into your derriere. Do both sides.

Rub your abdomen in a circular motion, pushing lightly in with your fingers as you do so.

Raise your legs. Knead them, working toward your heart.

Combine this with "Bathing Pleasures: Foot Bath."

Finish with your feet. Still lying down, put one knee up, and cross the other leg over it. Add oil to your hands, then rub them briskly together. Wrap your hands around your foot. Now, squeeze and pull the fleshy part between your toes. Knead the ball of your foot. Stroke the top and bottom of your foot lightly. Make a fist with your hand, and push hard into the arch.

See "Your Nurturing Voice," "Comfort Journal," and "Bathing Pleasures."

Experiment with making self-massage into a ritual. Talk to yourself with your nurturing voice. Use massage oil and candles to heighten the experience. Breathe deeply and concentrate on the sensations. Afterward try writing about your experience in your comfort journal. Combine with bathing pleasures.

Become Your Massage

Use self-massage to become a body part. Caress a part of your body that you like with a loving massage. Let your body part communicate with you. It may speak in movement or sounds or words. Listen to what it has to say. Concentrate on becoming the object of your loving attention.

If you enjoy this, try touching a part of your body you don't like. Keep your eyes closed, and just focus on touching and loving yourself, not judging.

More Self-Touching

Wash your face slowly with a textured washcloth and warm water.

Caress yourself with a large feather. Great before bed.

Make a fist, and run your knuckles over your arms and chest.

Roll a tennis ball under your bare feet.

Fill a basin with marbles, and roll different parts of your body on them.

Take a day to explore every texture you can. Choose a silk shirt to wear; pay attention to the feel of your makeup. Become an explorer of textures.

See "Comfort Clothing."

Touching Others

Talk to close friends about touching more. Discuss the different family and cultural messages you have all received about touching. Decide on a few specific ways to touch each other.

With friends, stand in a circle all facing one direction, and massage each other's backs. Concentrate on the caring that is uniting all of you. After a while, turn around and massage the person who was massaging you.

After a meal, give your meal mate a hand massage.

Wash your lover's hair outside in the sunshine.

See "Animal Antidotes" for more touching ideas.

Tickle a friend's arm.

RESOURCES:

The Listening Hand: Self-Healing Through the Rubenfeld Synergy Method of Talk and Touch, by Ilana Rubenfeld, with illustrations by Anne Kent Rush and Sylvia Plachy (Bantam, 2001). Integrates bodywork, intuition, talk, movement, awareness, imagination, humor, and compassionate touch as gateways to melt blocks in the body, mind, and emotions.

Energy Medicine, by Donna Eden (Jeremy Tarcher, 1999). A transformative, easy-to-learn treasury of healing.

Gentle Fitness, by Catherine MacRae (video). Self-massage demonstrated. Available on-line at various websites.

SELF-PLEASURING

What Is It?

None of us should be prohibited from experiencing the pleasure of sexual release. It is something we need and enjoy. It makes us feel better when we're blue. It is just as important as enjoying our work, taking care of our bodies, or living in a pleasant and safe environment. Loving self-pleasure makes us feel good about ourselves and the world.

You'll Need:

Sexual fantasies.

Sexy books or films.

A vibrator (optional). Some experts believe they make you less sensitive; others swear by them. The choice is yours.

Massage oil or lubricating jelly.

Pieces of silk, leather, terry cloth, feathers.

A sensual place to relax in.

When to Do It:

- When you pine for sexual release.
- If you have always wanted to try self-pleasuring or want to improve your present sexual repertoire.
- If you feel a tremendous amount of guilt and fear about the idea of touching yourself "down there."

What to Do:

Did You Know?

Sex needs to be learned and practiced. Because the human brain is so complex, humans are much less instinctive concerning sex.

Sex is influenced by your culture. Margaret Mead discovered that in women the potential for orgasm is strongly influenced by whether the dominant members of the culture consider women's pleasure important. Where women's pleasure is not valued, women are much less orgasmic.

Your clitoris has no other biological function than to provide you with sexual pleasure. God, Goddess, or evolution provided us with our clitoris solely for sexual pleasure.

Did you know? *Self-pleasuring ritual*

Fantasizing about someone other than your partner is completely natural and healthy. If we are in a committed relationship, it can actually help us stay put by allowing us variety and excitement in our minds.

Your vagina is considerably cleaner than your mouth.

The more orgasms you have, the more easily and frequently you will have them. In addition, self-pleasuring helps you learn what you like. If you don't know what feels good, how can you tell your partner?

Self-Pleasuring Ritual

You may have noticed I've gotten rid of the word *masturbate*. It is guilt inducing and harsh. Let's self-pleasure instead and leave the guilt behind.

See "Creative Selfishness" for help dealing with guilt.

Set aside an hour. An entire evening would be great. Don't rush this!

Prepare your bedroom (or any other private place) as if a lover were coming for a visit. Create a beautiful, sexy, relaxing environment. Switch your answering machine on. Light candles, play music that helps you feel sexy. Perfume the air with jasmine, rose, neroli, or ylang-ylang essential oils, pull out soft sheets, add exciting textures. Perhaps a glass of sparkling apple juice or champagne, a piece of chocolate, and a juicy peach for the bedside? To add a sacred element, you could adapt the blessing ritual in "Comfort Rituals" and bless your space for self-pleasuring. Be creative. Allow your fantasies to come true for you.

Pour some fragrant oil into your bath. Sink into the hot water, and *let go*. Entertain yourself with a fantasy. You could recall a sexy scene from a movie or make up a story. Whisper to yourself all the secret things that turn you on. Gently let your hands slide over your body. If you feel self-conscious, use a washcloth. Linger on the edge of excitement. No pressure, just anticipation.

See "Sweet Scents" and "Body Delights: Radiance."

When you are ready, rise slowly out of the tub and lovingly dry yourself off. Tease yourself with your towel by perhaps running it through your legs briskly or across your nipples. Use your nurturing voice to tell you great

See "Your Nurturing Voice."

things about yourself. You are a magnificent, one-of-a-kind woman. You are wonderful.

Retreat to your special space. Take a moment to appreciate the sensual environment you created *for yourself*. Entertain a few of your senses now. Touch sensual items around you. Let your body be in the moment.

Close your eyes, and recall a sexual experience in which you felt secure, sexy, and loved. Enter into your wonderful memory as fully as possible. Feel all the sensations in your body. Now rub your hands together rapidly. Imagine that you are filling them with divine energy and love. Lay your hands on your stomach or neck. Feel the warmth and energy. Touch yourself with your electric fingers. Lightly run your fingers up and down your body. You deserve pleasure.

Stay with your memory of your good loving time while your hands slide over your stomach and through your public hair. Flutter your fingers over your nipples. Tease yourself; don't be in a hurry. Now, drop a little oil onto your fingers. Run your hands quickly up and down your body. That lover in your memory is now you. Say "I love you" in your sexiest voice. Slide your silky hand over your mound and over your vagina. Imagine these are the petals of a beautiful flower that belong solely to you. Gently slip a finger inside your vagina.

Make quick circles around your clitoris, brushing up against it lightly. Touch your clitoris and your nipples at the same time. Try holding your clitoris between your thumb and index finger. Learn which part of your clitoris is most sensitive. Experiment with different strokes. Let yourself go!

Over time, as you pleasure yourself, experiment with coming close to orgasm and then stopping. Stroke your belly and pelvis. Imagine the warmth you feel spreading slowly up and out, down your legs and up into your womb and stomach. When you begin to calm down, start exciting yourself again. When you get close to coming again, stop and caress the area around your heart, then up your throat. Continue until you feel that you have spread your sexual energy throughout your entire body. Let yourself have an orgasm to end all orgasms.

The point of self-pleasuring is to feel good. Luxuriate in a sense of celebration for your body. If you feel self-conscious, go back to stroking safe areas and focus on the good sex memory. It can also be great fun to read a sexy book or watch a wild video at this point.

Vibrators come in all shapes and sizes. They can help if you are having a difficult time enjoying yourself. If you feel nothing and become bored or frustrated, stop. Try again in a few days. But don't give up. Compare what you feel when you touch your clitoris to what you feel when you touch your knee. I bet there is a difference. Keep going, and the difference will become huge!

RESOURCES:

Sex for One, by Betty Dodson (Crown, 1996). A raucous celebration of self-pleasuring.

Erotic Interludes, edited by Lonnie Garfield Barbach (Penguin, 1995). Erotica that doesn't degrade women.

Naughty Stories from A to Z, edited by Alison Tyler (Pretty Things Press, 2002). An unusual collection of red-hot stories that cover an assortment of sexual genres.

The Clitourist, by Karen Salmansohn, with illustrations by Trisha Krauss (Universe, 2002). True or false? The clitoris is the only organ found on either men or women that exists solely for pleasure, and many scientists believe women's genitals are more highly evolved than men's. True!

Best Women's Erotica, edited by Marcy Sheiner (Cleis Press, 2000). Literary steam.

Websites:

Clean Sheets
http://www.cleansheets.com

Nerve
http://www.nerve.com

BODY DELIGHTS

What Is It?

All of us know that exercise is good for us. It can lift us out of depression, put our problems in perspective, and make us feel more connected to our bodies. But can it also be fun and comforting?

You'll Need:

Shoes you can move in.

Music you can move to.

When to Do It:

- When you feel sluggish and wormlike.
- When you feel you are exercising in a self-abusive style.
- When you would like to explore exercise, but it seems too difficult, overwhelming, or boring.
- If people (including yourself) have always told you you were too big or clumsy to dance or do gymnastics or . . .

What to Do:

Feel Your Exercise

Focus on how you feel during an activity. As you walk, take turns concentrating on what your hands feel like, then your legs, then your neck, and so on. Feel your body coil and uncoil as you spring on a minitramp. Listen to your breath as you swim. Listen to the sound of the tennis ball hitting your racket. Let yourself enjoy the moment.

A Short Walk

After dinner, take a walk with your kids, your lover, or just you and the moon. Watch the stars, play hide-and-seek behind trees, chase fireflies.

Stretch Gardening

Make gardening a dance. S-t-r-e-t-c-h for each weed, leap between flower beds, pirouette on the lawn. (This one probably works best in the backyard.)

Feel your exercise
A short walk
Stretch gardening
Greet the day, end the day
Get sweaty
Take it all in
Whirling dervish
Wild thing
Radiance

Greet the Day, End the Day

Dance at dawn to reggae music while you watch the sun rise. Boogie naked in the moonlight to big band tunes. Feel the music.

Get Sweaty

Go for a brisk walk carrying two-pound weights. Ride a bike fast and furiously. Rent an aerobic workout tape, and go home and do it. Put on *Graceland* by Paul Simon or *The Neighborhood* by Los Lobos or *Slavonic Dances* by Dvořák, and dance, skip, hop, twist, and shout. Let your frustrations, your passions, your energy out!

Take It All In

Get a massage. As the masseuse manipulates your body, concentrate on accepting the attention. Breathe away your nervousness at having someone touch you. Close your eyes, and imagine the masseuse sending you healing energy. Direct this energy to where you are tense or sore. Allow yourself to be the center of attention. Take, and don't worry about giving anything back. You deserve all this attention. You are worth it.

Whirling Dervish

Find a large space. Dress in flowing clothing. Play wild music. Throw your arms and hands out. Stand on the toes of one foot, and push off with the other in a counterclockwise movement. Keep pushing, moving faster and faster. Let your cares and worries fly away from you.

Wild Thing

This is great for letting go of anger and frustration. Spontaneously, quickly, pick something wild—animal, person, or spirit, Amazon queen, wind, or lion. Turn on some fierce music. Move into your role by imitating your being's movements. Stomp, gnash your teeth, or make wild noises. Let your muscles express your suppressed feelings. Rage, stretch, contract, growl, fight, leap—become a wild thing. Propel yourself into your role while staying connected to how your body feels. Notice your breathing, your movements, your tone of voice. Play until you are spent. Collapse.

Radiance

Imagine there is a magic lightbulb inside of you, near your navel. Sit quietly. Click the lightbulb on. Feel the glow start within you. The bulb begins to heat up and emits a living, pulsating warmth. You feel the light beams moving throughout your entire body, up through your chest and out along your arms. Each of your fingers glows with radiant light.

Feel the heat course up your neck, into your head and face. Your brain is now alive with brilliant magic light. Your eyes begin to glow, emitting this beautiful inner light for all to see.

Now the light beams travel down, along your spine and into your womb, filling you with a pleasant warmth. The glow glides into your thighs, your calves, and finally your feet. Each of your toes blazes with light.

Stand up. You are filled with energy. Your magic light radiates power into everything you do today. Throughout the day, go back to your center and remember your magic lightbulb, emitting pure energy and spine-tingling warmth.

See "Self-Pleasuring."

This is a great visualization to do before an exercise workout or to get yourself in the mood to exercise. It can also be used in conjunction with self-pleasuring or shared with a partner before or during sex.

RESOURCES:

Relaxercise, by David Zemach-Bersin, Kaethe Zemach-Bersin, and Mark Reese (HarperSanFrancisco, 1990). Tension-releasing exercises that worked miracles on my clenched jaw.

Well Being: Rejuvenating Recipes for Body and Soul, by Barbara Close (Chronicle Books, 2000). A gorgeous and useful book with recipes for all kinds of luxurious botanical body potions and treats.

The Woman's Book of Yoga and Health: A Lifelong Guide to Wellness, by Linda Sparrowe and Patricia Walden, with photos by David Martinez

(Shambhala, 2002). To me, the best book on yoga and women's health in print.

The Anatomy of Change: A Way to Move Through Life's Transition, by Richard Strozzi Heckler (North Atlantic Books, 1993). Heckler uses aikido to help us live in our bodies in ways that create new possibilities. Very powerful.

Intuitive Body: Aikido as a Clairsentient Practice, by Wendy Palmer (North Atlantic Books, 2000). Palmer works from the same aikido base as Heckler—they were once married—revealing her own insights into creating a body that can respond to life by returning to center.

The Pilates Body: The Ultimate At-Home Guide to Strengthening, Lengthening, and Toning Your Body—Without Machines, by Brooke Siler (Broadway Books, 2000). The focus of this exercise is on the abdominals, which support the back. It is a good introduction to Pilates.

Relax into Stretch: Instant Flexibility Through Mastering Muscle Tension, by Pavel Tsatsouline (video). Easy-to-understand stretching techniques.

Bellydance Fitness for Beginners (Gold Home Media, 2001). A series of videotapes or DVDs, including basic moves, arms and abs, hips, buns and thighs. A fun way to escape from the ordinary aerobic workout!

Music

Music for Energy and Motivation by Steven Mark Kohn, *GEMS* by Patti La Belle, *Individuality* by Rachelle, *A Rose Is Still a Rose* by Aretha Franklin, "Jupiter" from Gustav Holst's symphony *The Planets*.

Websites:

Beginning Guide to Fitness
http://www.ladyoracle.com/lifeguides.html

Take a Break Online
http://www.takeabreakonline.com

Yoga Journal
http://www.yogajournal.com

Lush
http://www.lush.com

BATHING PLEASURES

What Is It?

You slip into a sparkling tub filled to the brim with hot water. Fragrant smells caress your nose, candlelight dances off the walls, water lilies float among iridescent bubbles. . . . Water is the great purifier of life. But there is more than one way to take a bath!

You'll Need:

A private bathtub and shower.

Essential oils, herbs, favorite perfumes, shower gels.

Candles. Flowers. Beautiful potted plants.

Fluffy cotton towels.

Music that delights and soothes you.

When to Do It:

- When it is raining and cold outside or humid and hot.
- When your back aches.
- When you are fighting off a cold.
- Any time you would naturally retreat to the bathtub.

What to Do:

A Bathing Ritual

Prepare your bathroom for bathing. Light your candles. Place a flower or plant near the water.

Start with a brief, warm shower. Using a loofah or bathing brush with a shower gel or soft soap, scrub your body. Rinse off in cool water.

Towel off briskly, and slip into a soft, clean robe.

Fill your clean tub with hot water. Add the scent of the day. Consider floating flowers on the water.

While your tub is filling, sit quietly. Concentrate on your breathing.

Step outside the bathroom and announce, "I am leaving the world out here." Close the door firmly behind you.

A bathing ritual | *Hand bath*
Shower in the dark | *Salt bath*
Foot bath | *Waterfall visualization*

Start your music now.

Let your nurturing voice say good things about your body as you slip into the water.

See "Your Nurturing Voice."

Study a candle flame. Trace the edge of a leaf. Contemplate the color of a flower. Meditate. Do a deep stretch. Play with the water. Rub yourself all over with a square of silk. Touch and pleasure yourself. Play with bath toys. Just be in the primordial warmth of your bath.

When you are finished, pull the drain, stand up, and recite, "Everything negative in my life is now washing down the drain."

Shower in the Dark

Showering in the dark is a wonderful way to relieve sensory overload. Imagine this as a way to wipe your mind clean.

This shower works best in total darkness. If you are afraid of falling, add a candle or use a night-light.

Concentrate solely on the sensual pleasures of the water. Shut out everything else.

Foot Bath

Fill a basin with warm water. Add chamomile tea to the water for a soothing effect or a teaspoon of cayenne pepper for rejuvenation. Play some upbeat music. Slip your feet into the water. Sip wine or herbal tea. **Relax.** Thank your feet for supporting you. Let your body's energy replenish itself.

See "Touch: A Self-Massage" for a foot massage.

Hand Bath

Soak your hands in hot water. Add a drop of rosemary or sage essential oil. Massage your hands and rotate your wrists while you soak. Also try soaking your hands in warmed olive oil.

See "Sweet Scents: Aromatherapy" for essential oil info.

Salt Bath

This bath roughly approximates the feeling of a floatation tank. Fill your tub with warm, not hot, water. Add coarse salt. Experiment with the amount, starting with two cups, until you achieve good buoyancy.

Bathe in the dark. Play music that sounds primordial and mystical. Another idea is to add kelp to the water. You will feel like you are floating in the ocean.

Waterfall Visualization

Combine this visualization with a shower, or use it alone.

Relax.

Imagine yourself in a lush tropical rain forest. All around you, exotic birds make magical music. Soft, warm sunlight flickers through tall trees. There is a stream near your feet. You follow the stream until it leads you to a tranquil pool. At the far edge of the pool is a gentle waterfall, surrounded by a balmy mist.

You slip out of what you are wearing and step into the pool. The water is the perfect temperature. You wade until you are under the waterfall.

Relaxing totally, you let the water wash over you. It washes away all your tensions, all your worries, all your gloomy feelings. This is a magical waterfall, and it fills you with a wonderful feeling of well-being. It nurtures every cell in your body until you tingle all over. Stay here as long as you need, washing away all your stress, all your anxiety.

Whenever you are ready, you slip back to shore and into your clothes. Finally, you gently float back to consciousness.

Open your eyes and bask in your feeling of well-being and buoyant energy.

RESOURCES:

Water Magic, by Mary Muryn and Cathy Cash Spellman (Fireside, 1995). Fabulous!

SWEET SCENTS

What Is It?

Scented sheets, roast turkey with gravy, a freshly fragrant bedroom: Aromas have an incredible power to connect us with memories, calm our minds, and thaw our neglected spirits. Our sense of smell is too powerful a comfort tool to neglect.

You'll Need:

Your nose.

Various botanical ingredients, including essential oils and herbs.

An eyedropper.

When to Do It:

- If you neglect the power of scent in your life.
- If any of your pleasant memories are triggered by familiar smells.
- If your life literally stinks.

What to Do:

Scent Exploration

Devote a week to learning what smells you like. Make notes in your comfort journal. You can usually only experiment for a few minutes before your nose gets tired. As you smell something, say to yourself, "This is the smell of a pine tree." Be as specific as possible.

Take a smell stroll through a five-and-dime store, by an ocean, into an Italian restaurant, by a wharf, into a specialty grocery, or through the woods just as it starts to rain. Try this at different times of the day. Early morning is especially nice.

Recreating Smells from Childhood

Relax. Close your eyes. In your mind, picture yourself as a child. Pick any age. Reassure your child self that she is safe. Ask her to help you remember comforting smells. Allow your younger self to walk around your parent or

---

Scent exploration
Recreating smells from childhood
Scented flowers and plants
Aromatherapy
Baths
Whiffs
Massage oils
Bath oils
Making nice smells for your home

grandparent's house, out into the yard, around your grade school, through your favorite playground. Take a deep sniff. Focus on remembering pleasurable scents. Compile a mental aroma list. When you are ready, gently open your eyes and record your favorite smells in your comfort journal.

If this doesn't bring back any memories of comforting scents, try sniffing a few popular favorites: White Shoulders or Chanel No. 5 cologne, baby powder, vanilla, a new book, lilacs, freshly cut grass, newly turned dirt, dill pickles, onions and garlic frying in olive oil, old leather, the smell of the ocean, bread baking, cotton candy, popcorn, burgers on the grill, pine boughs, coffee brewing, and bacon sizzling.

Schedule an hour or two to stock up on your familiar smells. Fill your house, work, and car with emergency smell stashes. A sample vial of Chanel No. 5 might rest in your glove compartment for a soothing sniff during a traffic jam. Try cooking for smell when you are down. If an aroma can't be stocked, go after that scent when you need comfort. Take a walk and sniff for newly mowed grass, wood smoke, or dinner cooking.

Scented Flowers and Plants

See "Green Things" for planting help and buying info.

Force Soleil d'Or narcissi, freesia, or grape hyacinth bulbs in your office. Sage, rosemary, and French lavender love dry, sunny conditions and should grow easily in pots in your kitchen. Fill a window box or container outside your bedroom window with sweet rocket, white sage, golden flame honeysuckle, Chilean jasmine, night-scented stocks, *Nicotiana affinis*, or evening primrose. All of these plants release a wonderful scent at night. Just open your window to scent your room. Mock orange shrub, lily of the valley, and sweet alyssum can be grown near your front door to welcome you home with their sweet smells. For indoor scented plants, try almond, lemon, rose, or peppermint scented geraniums. When choosing bulbs, seeds, or plants, look for nonhybrid types. The older, plainer plants tend to smell better.

Aromatherapy

Aromatherapy is the art of using essential oils (highly aromatic and concentrated substances distilled from plants and herbs) to heal and enhance your life. Essential oils are rarely used in their undiluted form. They are usually mixed with oils, alcohol, or water.

Warning: Essential oils can be fatal. Keep out of reach of children. Test a small drop on the inside of your arm before using all over your body. When trying unfamiliar ones, check with a reputable source first. All recipes below are safe for external use only.

Baths

See "Bathing Pleasures."

It is a good idea the first time you use an oil in your bath to use only two or three drops. Some oils can irritate your skin. You can increase or decrease the amounts as you experiment to find out what works best for you.

To relax after a hard day, add 3 drops of lavender and 2 drops of tangerine oil or try 3 drops of geranium oil.

To warm up before a sexy encounter with your partner or a self-pleasuring ritual, add 2 drops ylang-ylang, 2 drops jasmine, and 3 drops sandalwood oil to a warm bath. Rose oil and clary sage are also considered aphrodisiacs.

To sooth your tender self and get relief from premenstrual syndrome, try 2 drops mugwort and 2 drops sandalwood oil in warm to hot water. (Don't use mugwort if you're pregnant, but then you wouldn't have PMS, would you?)

Three drops of clary sage, 2 of marjoram, and 1 of peppermint in a warm to hot bath can help relieve cramps caused by your period.

To help prevent a cold, try 2 drops of lavender, 2 drops bergamot, and 2 drops tea tree oil in a hot bath or 2 drops juniper, 1 drop pepper oil, and 3 drops of lavender in a warm to hot bath.

To pick you up when you are depressed, mix 3 drops rose and 2 drops lavender oil into a warm bath.

For a pick-me-up bath before a big night out, soak in 2 drops of rosemary and rosewood or 2 drops rosemary and 2 of bergamot in tepid to warm water.

For an invigorating morning bath, try 2 drops rosemary, 2 drops juniper oil, and 1 drop peppermint in tepid to warm water.

A hot bath with 2 drops of ylang-ylang and 2 drops of lavender can help relieve jet lag and promote sleep.

See "Touch: A Self-Massage" for a foot massage.

Four drops of peppermint oil or 3 drops of juniper oil, 2 of lavender, and 1 of rosemary in a foot bath can help aching feet. Combine with a foot massage.

A hot bath with 5 drops of lavender an hour before bed followed by 1 drop of neroli on a tissue by your pillow can help you beat insomnia.

A hot bath with 2 drops chamomile, 4 drops lavender, and 2 drops orange blossom right before bed will help you sleep.

Whiffs

A drop of basil oil on a tissue or straight from the bottle revives your brain.

A whiff of peppermint can calm a queasy stomach.

The smell of lavender, neroli, lemongrass, or linden blossom can calm you and help you sleep. Keep a bottle by your bed, and when you can't sleep try a drop on a tissue.

Massage Oils

Add 2 drops geranium, jasmine, lavender, or rose to 2 ounces of sweet almond oil for help relieving depression or anxiety.

Try adding 5 drops eucalyptus oil to 2 ounces sweet almond oil. Rub it sparingly on your throat and chest during a cold, or add it to a bath. Peppermint, rosemary, and marjoram are also helpful for colds.

For sore muscles, cramps, or lower back pain, take 2 ounces almond oil and add 6 drops of chamomile, 4 drops clary sage, and 4 drops marjoram essential oils or 5 drops of juniper, 4 drops lavender, and 4 drops rosemary to 2 ounces of almond oil or 5 drops of clary sage and 3 drops of rosemary to 2 ounces of almond oil. Gently massage the sore areas.

For an aphrodisiac massage oil, try 3 drops of jasmine, 3 drops of rose, 5 drops of sandalwood, and 3 drops of bergamot to 2 ounces of the base oil of your choice.

A massage oil that is supposed to help stretch marks consists of 8 drops of lavender and 3 drops of neroli to 2 ounces of wheat germ oil.

Bath Oils

Use a base oil of avocado, sunflower, wheat germ, or sweet almond oil. For every 2 ounces of base oil, add 5 to 10 drops of essential oil. As when bathing with essential oils, start with fewer drops and work up. Use any of the bathing or massage oil recipes, and experiment with new combinations. Pour the base oil into a clean bottle, and add essential oil(s). If you want bubbles, add a half ounce of your favorite unscented organic cleanser. For more bubbles, use only the cleanser and no oil. Cap the bottle and shake well. Add to your bath for a sensual experience.

Making Nice Smells for Your Home

Put a drop of your favorite scent in your vacuum cleaner bag.

Put 2 drops of your favorite oil in a shallow bowl of warm water.

Dampen a tissue with 2 or 3 drops of ylang-ylang, patchouli, geranium, linden blossom, or rose, then wrap this tissue in a piece of cloth and tuck in with your clothes. (Don't put the oil directly on your clothes, because some oils stain.)

Place 2 drops of your favorite essential oil on a metal ring, then rest the ring on a lightbulb and turn the light on. Terra-cotta rings also work.

Tuck sachets in your car, briefcase, or desk or between your sheets.

Hang a small cotton bag of lavender from your rearview mirror, and experience more calming drives.

Burn fragrant grasses in a fireplace. Experiment with burning different types of wood. Piñon pine is especially nice.

Avoid air fresheners of all kinds. They coat your nose with chemicals to deaden your sense of smell. Also try eliminating strong-smelling detergents. They can be harmful to the environment, and they deaden your sense of smell.

RESOURCES:

The Complete Book of Essential Oils and Aromatherapy, by Valerie Ann Worwood (New World Library, 1991). A great all-around resource.

Aromatherapy for Healing the Spirit: Restoring Emotional and Mental Balance with Essential Oils, by Gabriel Mojay (Healing Arts Press, 2000). Guidance for a wide range of emotional and mental complaints.

The Scented Room: Cherchez's Book of Dried Flowers, Fragrance, and Potpourri, by Barbara Milo Ohrbach, with photographs by Joe Standart and Anne Marie Cloutier (Clarkson Potter, 1986). A classic resource.

Clean House, Clean Planet: Clean Your House for Pennies a Day, the Safe, Nontoxic Way, by Karen Noonan Logan (Pocket, 1997). Keep toxic odors out, and create simple clean smells and good health, too.

HERBAL HELP

What Is It?

A wise old crone stands over a boiling cauldron. The firelight dances in her long silver hair. The smell of pungent herbs fills the air as she brews an herbal tea for your menstrual cramps. . . . Blink your eyes, and it is you, standing in your well-lit kitchen, preparing a healing herbal mixture. Try the venerable art of using herbs and other organic ingredients for healing yourself. You'll make a comforting connection to women's past as healers, and you'll care for yourself with effective, natural prescriptions.

You'll Need:

Various herbs.

A tea infuser and ceramic or porcelain pot.

Small muslin bags or old clean cotton socks.

When to Do It:

- When you feel like creating with natural ingredients.
- When you want to try natural help for sleeplessness, cramps, headaches, and so on.

What to Do:

All the recipes in this section are made using dried herbs, which are easier to find than you think. Check health food stores, your phone directory under "Herbs," ethnic grocery stores, or mail order sources.

Herbal Bathing Concoctions

You can make a herbal bath by infusion. To make an infusion, put the proper amount of herbs in one quart of water, bring to a boil, then simmer, covered, for about fifteen minutes. Strain and pour the liquid in your bath water. The remaining solid residue can be wrapped in a washcloth and used to rub your body.

You can also put the dried herbs of your choice in a cotton sock or small muslin bag, tie this over the tub faucet, and turn on the water. Or you can simply float the bag in your bathwater.

Tense? Heat up a bathing infusion from 2 ounces of lemon balm leaves or chamomile, or fill a sock with 1 ounce each of thyme, sage, and lavender.

Herbal bathing concoctions *Sleep pillows*
Making herbal teas

Burned out from thinking too hard at work or school? Drop a cotton sock filled with 1 ounce each of pine and peppermint or 2 ounces rosemary into your tub.

After a hard workout or to soothe aches brought on by the flu, take 1 heaping tablespoon each of rosemary, chamomile, peppermint, thyme, and yarrow. Make an infusion of all the above ingredients. Strain and add to a warm bath. Also great for a foot bath.

To recharge your batteries, try running a bath with 1 tablespoon each of patchouli, geranium leaf, mint, orange leaf, sage, strawberry leaf, woodruff, and rosemary in a cotton sock.

One heaping tablespoon each of lavender, rosemary, comfrey, and thyme in a bath bag is a lovely, all-purpose comfort potion.

Making Herbal Teas

To make the teas, put the recommended amount of herb in the bottom of your teapot. Cover with boiling water. Put the lid on for ten minutes. Strain the mixture as you pour. You can also put the herbs inside a tea infuser and simply remove the infuser after ten minutes.

You can add honey and lemon to any of these teas.

To help you relax and sleep:

1/4 teaspoon lavender flowers
1/2 teaspoon lemon balm leaves
1/2 teaspoon linden flowers (also known as lime blossoms)
1/2 teaspoon chamomile

or

1/2 teaspoon valerian root
1/2 teaspoon passionflowers
1/2 teaspoon chamomile
1/2 teaspoon vervain

or

1 teaspoon yerba buena
1 teaspoon spearmint

For bad-tasting but effective cramp and PMS relief, try:

$^1/_2$ teaspoon chamomile
$^1/_2$ teaspoon cramp bark
$^1/_2$ teaspoon wild yam
$^1/_2$ teaspoon grated ginger root

For a refreshing pick-up:

$^1/_2$ teaspoon rose hips
$^1/_2$ teaspoon peppermint
$^1/_2$ teaspoon hibiscus

For help with a cold, try:

1 teaspoon wintergreen
1 teaspoon lemon verbena

or

1 teaspoon yarrow
1 teaspoon valerian
1 teaspoon birch leaf

Goldenseal tastes terrible but also helps relieve colds.

Sleep Pillows

Try mixing 2 ounces rose petals, 1 ounce mint, 1 ounce rosemary, and a tissue with a few drops of clove oil on it. Stuff into a muslin bag, then tuck or sew into a pillow. Rest on this pillow whenever you have trouble sleeping.

Another calming mixture can be made from 2 ounces agrimony, 1 ounce woodruff, 1 ounce crushed cloves, 1 ounce crushed and dried orange peel, 1 ounce orris root powder, and 2 drops orange oil.

To help you remember your dreams, tuck 8 ounces of mugwort into your pillow.

RESOURCES:

Herbs for Health and Healing, by Kathi Keville with Peter Korn (Berkeley Books, 1996). A comprehensive pocket sourcebook for herbal treatment for a multitude of ailments. Includes a cooking guide with recipes, a special chapter on aromatherapy, and a complete handbook to herbal health and healing.

Women's Herbs, Women's Health, by Christopher Hobbs and Kathi Keville (Interweave Press, 1998). More focused than *Herbs for Health and Healing,* this book discusses in detail fourteen of the most common health problems facing women today, including PMS, urinary tract infections, sexually transmitted diseases, mood disorders, osteoporosis, menopause, cervical dysplasia, and heart disease.

Herbal Healing for Women: Simple Home Remedies for Women of All Ages, by Rosemary Gladstar (Fireside, 1993). Another comprehensive and easy-to-use guide. Explains how to create remedies—including teas, tinctures, salves, and ointments—for the common disorders that arise in the different cycles of a woman's life.

The Herbal Tea Garden: Planning, Planting, Harvesting, and Brewing, by Marietta Marshall Marcin (Storey Books, 1993). For the gardener and herbal tea lover. A complete handbook for selecting, growing, and brewing herbs.

The Herbal Home Spa: Naturally Refreshing Wraps, Rubs, Lotions, Masks, Oils, by Greta Breedlove (Storey Books, 1998). One of several great source books.

AESTHETIC PLEASURES

What Is It?

The age-old practice of nurturing ourselves with culture and aesthetics provides tremendous resources when we need comfort. To be diverted from our problems and have our spirits touched by brilliance at the same time is potent comfort indeed.

You'll Need:

Art museums and galleries.

Crafts that interest you.

Art books, photography books, books about artists' lives.

When to Do It:

- When you are depressed by your physical environment.
- When you need inspiration for a project or creative endeavor.
- When you get that dragged down, the-world-is-an-ugly-place feeling.

What to Do:

Museums and Galleries

Walk in with confidence. You own the place. Don't allow anyone to intimidate you. If there is a catalog or map, study it for the exhibits that interest you. *See only what you like.* You do not have to see everything! That could end up depressing instead of comforting you.

Stand very close to a painting, then stand far away. Squint at it. Study the details with opera glasses. Sketch the outline without looking at your paper. Notice color, shadow, facial expressions. Trust yourself to know what you like, not what you are supposed to like. Avoid making verbal, rational connections with the image. Try to allow your unconscious mind and spirit to connect to the images and shapes.

Pay attention to the outside of a museum. You may find peaceful gardens, sculpture, or wonderful architectural elements to please you.

Museums and galleries *Cultural*
Inspiration *Make beauty*

Immerse yourself in the life of a favorite artist. Visit a museum to see her work. Read a book about her life. Buy a poster or postcards to decorate your personal sanctuary. Read the books she read, view the paintings of her friends, learn about the culture she lived in.

See "A Personal Sanctuary."

See "A Self-Care Schedule."

Pick several comforting or inspiring works of art at a museum near you. Schedule regular visits to these favorites. Try sitting in front of an especially nurturing work of art for twenty or thirty minutes, while writing down all your thoughts and feelings.

Look for unusual or out-of-the-way art experiences. A university gallery, a small art school exhibit, a private collection, or a historical home tour can provide rare pleasures.

Inspiration

Collect aesthetic sources to keep around your home or office. Rhonda Foreman, an art educator, photographer, and mother, told me about a pin board she keeps near her desk upon which she displays art postcards, quotes, strange headlines, small posters, and found objects. She finds inspiration as well as solace when she's stuck: she rearranges the images, creating refreshing juxtapositions. Try putting a board like this near your desk, dining room table, or where you talk on the phone.

Stacks of art books are common in artists' work spaces. What about art books for your office desk or piled near your bed? Writing a report, trying to sleep, nursing your baby, you can let images speak to you. Art books are expensive. Find a lending library that specializes in art books; mention titles to friends and family as gift suggestions; budget books as a priority.

Next time you're stuck on a project or life seems stale, stroll through a part of your town known for its display windows. Melrose Avenue in Los Angeles is a great example. Instead of regarding the displays as filled with objects to possess, view the objects as art in a gallery.

Cultural

Order poetry on tape. A good reading will make poetry much more accessible. Get together with several friends. Each of you can order a tape and then trade later.

Attend a cultural experience you have never tried before. Modern ballet, Italian opera, Kabuki theater, the neighborhood playhouse, a string quartet, Cajun music, jazz, a Beethoven symphony. . . .

What about taking a workshop in acting, painting, or creating jewelry?

Culture doesn't have to be expensive. Even small towns offer regular lectures, gallery exhibits, local theater, lunchtime concerts, and radio drama that are free or inexpensive. Be a detective, and ferret out these cultural experiences.

Make Beauty

Hand-tint black-and-white photographs. Take the photos yourself, or buy a few in a junk shop. Use photo tinting oils, which are available at large art supply stores. They are coloring books for grown-ups.

Paint or refinish furniture. The sweaty work involved can be very absorbing, and the sense of pride at the transformation you brought about, uplifting.

Paint your face with makeup or nontoxic paints like those clowns use. Express your inner self or your current mood.

Find a shallow, sturdy box, roughly the size and depth of a medium-sized picture frame. Fill it with clean white builder's sand. Comb patterns, shapes, lines in the sand. Use it as a centerpiece and change it every day to fit your frame of mind.

The key to making beauty is not to get overwhelmed. Don't sabotage yourself by attempting too big a project or thinking it must turn out perfect. Make your goal immersion in the task at hand. Allow your creative spirit some time out of her closet. Gain an appreciation for what it takes to be an artist. If you also create an object of beauty, appreciate it as an extra dividend.

RESOURCES:

Sister Wendy's 1,000 Masterpieces, by Wendy Beckett (Dorling Kindersley Publishing, 1999). Unlock art with this unsurpassed anthology of Western art from one of the best-loved art historians.

The Quiet Eye: A Way of Looking at Pictures, by Sylvia Shaw Judson (Regnery Publishing, 1988). Feed your spirit through your eyes.

Artist at Work: Inside the Studios of Today's Most Celebrated Artists, by David Seidner (Rizzoli International). Go inside the studios of the most important artists of our time.

Writers on Artists, edited by A. S. Byatt (Dorling Kindersley Publishing, 2001). Brings together the best and brightest of the art and literary worlds. Features rare interviews and over 350 stunning full-color reproductions of many rarely seen works.

Language of Life: A Festival of Poets, by Bill Moyers (Main Street Books, 1996). A series of fascinating conversations with thirty-four American poets about how they make poetry.

Websites:

National Public Radio
http://www.npr.org

World Wide Art Resources
http://wwar.com

Art Museum Websites and Research Centers
http://www.lib.duke.edu/lilly/artsearch/guides/artmuseums.htm

Smithsonian
http://www.si.edu

Museums in the United States
http://www.museumca.org/usa

A Poem a Day
www.poems.com

Poetry 180
http://www.loc.gov/poetry/180

QUIET, PLEASE

What Is It?

Quiet is soothing, comforting, relaxing solace. But some sounds in your environment disturb this solace. Certain noises can make you uncomfortable, irritable, or angry. You can do something about them.

You'll Need:

Your ears.

Various sound-deadening items, like rugs, foam rubber, and earplugs.

When to Do It:

- When you find yourself battling headaches or feeling irritable because of the noises surrounding you.
- When you often remark, "If only I had a little peace and quiet. . . ."

What to Do:

Be a Sound Detective

Spend the next week listening carefully to the sounds around you. Several times throughout each day, stand still, close your eyes, and listen. What is the farthest noise you can discern? What is the closest? Be aware of the sounds when you awaken, during your workday, in the evening, on Saturday mornings. Notice your emotional reaction to sounds. Do you get irritable with your lover when the dishwasher is on? Does the early morning roar of the garbage truck usually herald a bad day? Become conscious of what sounds are around you, and then take steps to eliminate or improve them.

Eliminate Distressing Noises

Use carpeting, heavy drapes, and upholstered furniture to warm up your work space or home. Roller shades made out of heavy material will muffle noise from a street while insulating your room. If you hate wall-to-wall carpeting, use throw rugs or carpet remnants with padding underneath. Bookshelves on a wall between rooms will help insulate and prevent noise from traveling.

Don't compromise your performance at work because of noise stress. Acoustic screens, white noise machines, closed doors, earplugs, even a Walkman can quiet your work spot.

Be a sound detective
Eliminate distressing noises
Convert annoying noises

Quiet, Please

When suggesting changes to your boss, stress that your concentration, creativity, and performance will improve.

Place foam pads under blenders, mixers, food processors, typewriters, and computer printers to muffle the clatter.

When shopping for a new place to live, do the standing-still-with-eyes-closed test. Don't settle for uncomfortable or annoying noise levels if you can help it.

Consider installing a fountain, ceiling fan, or window air conditioner to mask annoying outside noise.

See "Nutritional Music."

Soothing music or environment sound recordings as background music can effectively mask unwanted noises. This can also work in a business situation.

Convert Annoying Noises

When you can't stop or block an offending noise, try imagining it as something else. Transform the hum of your refrigerator into a distant waterfall. Close your eyes and visualize a beautiful scene, perhaps in Hawaii or Brazil. Far in the distance, you can almost see foam exploding from a giant waterfall. The gentle hum of the refrigerator becomes the distant roar of this magnificent waterfall. Use your imagination to transform other annoying noises into soothing companions.

Another trick is to hum along with an offending noise. This works well with construction, heavy machinery, low-flying planes, crying babies, and traffic. Let's say a worker is jabbering away with a jackhammer underneath your office window. Mask the noise by quietly buzz-zz-zz-ing along. Match the pitch and intensity of your buzzing to the offending noise.

RESOURCE:

Creating the Not So Big House: Insights and Ideas for the New American Home, by Sarah Susanka, with photos by Grey Crawford (Taunton Press, 2002). Creating livable spaces.

SOOTHING SOUNDS

What Is It?

When you think of making noise for comfort, you might think of singing, tapping your feet, whistling, or humming. Those are great, but there are other ways to use your voice and simple musical instruments to release tension, lift up your mood, and energize your spirit.

You'll Need:

Your voice.

A small drum.

Chimes.

When to Do It:

- When you are so tense you think you might pop.
- If you have always wanted to make music.
- When you are out of balance or feeling at odds with yourself or someone else.
- If you often hum to yourself or make up little songs when you are happy or sad.

What to Do:

Toning

Elizabeth Keyes developed toning, the practice of allowing your body to speak, which helps you to release tension. The trick here is to allow yourself to let go. The more you can keep your conscious mind out of the experience, the better. It will probably seem a bit strange at first, but try it and see if it brings cleansing and comfort.

Stand with your feet about a foot apart and your knees unlocked. Imagine that a long string is attached to the top of your head and is elongating your spine. Loosen your jaw. Close your eyes. Listen to your breath. If you feel like it, sway gently from side to side. Focus on the flow of life throbbing through your body.

Toning	*Drumming*
Chanting	*Chimes*

Imagine a groan coming up from the soles of your feet. This is your body's voice, releasing pain, frustration, disappointments, everything unpleasant. Bring this groan up through your body. Open your mouth and exhale with a deep "ohh" or "ahh." Empty yourself. Allow your body to speak. Breathe from your abdomen. Continue to groan.

Continue sighing, wailing, groaning, or whatever comes out, whatever feels good, until you feel empty. Let out a deep sigh to finish. After toning, sit quietly for a few moments, observing how you feel, perhaps meditating or affirming how wonderful the coming day or evening will be.

During toning, you can concentrate on healing yourself or someone else by picturing the person in your mind.

Experiment with toning the next time you are angry, nervous, or experiencing a backache or indigestion. It may take a few tries before you feel truly comforted. See what happens.

Chanting

Chanting for both spiritual enlightenment and personal comfort enjoys a pedigree second to no other sound form. You naturally know how to chant. Whatever you do is perfectly correct. If you have never experienced chanting before, it may feel foreign or awkward the first few times. The first time I chanted, I was so self-conscious, my voice kept breaking. But after a few moments, I was able to relax and be carried away by the moving simplicity. Chanting is akin to singing yourself a lullaby. Play around, see if you like it, and know chanting has calmed people for centuries.

See "Nutritional Music: Personal Comfort Tape."

Devise a personal comfort chant. Pick simple and affirmative words. Examples could be, "I approve, I approve, I approve of myself"; "I'm safe, I'm safe, all is well in my world"; "I am myself, I am"; or "Peace, peace, peace, peace. May peace fill up my heart." You may want to use a comfort chant as part of other rituals. Try these and try making up your own.

Drumming

Drumming is another sound technique that lies outside our normal experience and yet is a truly effective method for soothing ourselves.

Imagine a dock with waves hitting the underpinnings. Hit your drum evenly, in time with the waves: one, two, three, four, one, two, three, four. Now one wave is larger and makes a harder thump when it hits the dock. Match this: ONE, two, three, four, ONE, two, three, four. Now every other wave is larger: ONE, two, THREE, four, ONE, two, THREE, four.

I use a little drum from the Taos Pueblo in New Mexico to do affirmations. I drum and sing one or two affirmations to comfort myself when I'm depressed or anxious. I have even used my drum to help me decide what my current goals are, a kind of spontaneous, personal rap song.

You will find that each drum has a voice of its own. Experiment with your drum and listen for its unique rhythm. Try warming hide drums over a fire or gas stove to bring out their true sound. Try beating your drum in different places: alone in the house, in the bathroom, in nature. It isn't scientific, it isn't performance; it is a simple and ancient way to calm and recharge yourself. Try chanting and drumming together.

Chimes

Playing chimes is similar to beating a drum in its timeworn simplicity, but the feelings it arouses are different. If drumming comforts the primal part of us, then chiming soothes our loftier, more ethereal self.

Carry small chimes with you. Play them when stuck in traffic, on your lunch break, in the bathtub. Experiment with different sequences, pitches, and volumes. Pay attention to the silence between chords. Again, this exceedingly simple act is amazingly powerful in its ability to bring you to a state of balanced, calm wonder.

RESOURCES:

Toning, by Elizabeth Keyes (Dimensions, 1979). You may obtain the book by writing to the publisher at P.O. Box 550, Marina Del Rey, CA 90294. Keyes's work has influenced many people.

The Way of Song: A Guide to Freeing the Voice and Sounding the Spirit, by Shawna Carol (St. Martin's Press, 2003). Be inspired to harness the power of the voice as a means of self-expression and spiritual growth using the SpiritSong method.

See "Nutritional Music: Resources" for more information.

NUTRITIONAL MUSIC

What Is It?

Most of us spend little time listening to music in a healing manner. It isn't something we are taught. (But then, we aren't taught to nurture ourselves either.) Music can heal and enhance your life in a myriad of ways. Open your ears and recognize music as the vital comfort tool it is!

You'll Need:

A stereo, tape, or CD player.

Music.

When to Do It:

- When you need healthy distractions from unpleasant thoughts.
- When your heart and soul need hugging.
- When you are depressed, tired, frazzled, or anxious.
- When you need a prod toward being creative.

What to Do:

A Sound Bath

Your entire body is sensitive to sound: your liver, the tiny membranes inside your lungs, your brain, your big toe.

Choose healing music like *Garden of Serenity* by David and Steve Gordon, *Shamanic Dream* by Anugama, "Air on a G-String" written by Bach, *Pilgrim Heart* by Krisha Das, or *Baroque at Bathtime* recorded by various artists.

Relax. Lie down with your feet near your speakers. Support your neck with a pillow. Imagine the music is water flowing around you, lifting you up, washing away all your tension. Let the music cradle you, enfold you, caress you.

When you are completely relaxed, allow the music to enter through the soles of your feet. Feel the music filling your feet. Allow it to move through your ankles, calves, thighs. Feel the vibrations inside you. Allow the music to

---

flow up your pelvis, into your stomach, lungs, out along your arms, tingling through each and every finger. Now feel the music filling your heart. Finally, the music courses through your neck and face, massaging each muscle, filling every fiber of your head with beauty and relaxation.

When the music is over, spend a few moments enjoying the feeling in your body. Experiment with different types of music on different days. Many subtle variations are possible.

See "Bathing Pleasures: Salt Bath"; "Soothing Sounds: Chanting"; and "A Day Off" for possibilities.

Try combining this exercise with one of the other rituals in the book.

Intensifying Your Mood

Pick a piece of music that matches your present mood. If you are tense, try "Vessel" from the *Koyannisqatsi* soundtrack by Phillip Glass. Happy? "Spring" from the *Four Seasons* by Vivaldi or *Cosmic Thing* by the B-52's. Fragile? *Heart to Heart* by Betty Buckley or *The Romance of the Violin* by Joshua Bell. Feeling creative? Listen to the *Fantasia* soundtrack. Needing to move? Put on *Totem* by Gabrielle Roth or *The Commitments: The Soundtrack*.

See "Letting off Steam," "Little Losses," "Self-Pleasuring," or "Bathing Pleasures."

As the music ends, imagine the last notes filling your body with gentle well-being. When you are ready, put on a meditative, spiritually nourishing selection like "Claire de Lune" by Debussy, *Walela* by Walela, *Shelter* by Rasa, or *Hush* by Jane Sieberry. Allow the music to fill your spirit. Let your body move spontaneously without thought or planning. Breath it into your heart, your back, your legs, out your hands. Receive.

Personal Comfort Tape

Create a comfort tape. It can feature your favorite nourishing music, affirmations, and messages of encouragement. Make the tape when you are feeling good, full of creative energy. Create an oral love letter to yourself. Other possibilities include getting people you trust to speak lovingly to you, recording comedy routines or even a great phone message someone left you. You could also try adding a poem or quotes to the recital.

Finding Music You Like

Music is very much a matter of individual taste. Start keeping a music notebook with selections listed under possible uses. Meditation music, music to get happy with, music to grieve with, whatever needs you have. Make notes whenever you hear something on the radio, on a movie soundtrack, at a friend's house.

To experiment with music before you buy, check out the largest public library in your area and record stores or bookstores that will allow you to listen to music before you buy.

RESOURCES:

The Power of Sound: How to Manage Your Personal Soundscape for a Vital, Productive, and Healthy Life, by Joshua Leeds

The Roar of Silence: Healing Powers of Breath, Tone, and Music, by Don G. Campbell (Theosophical Publishing, 1989). A modern pioneer in using sound to heal.

Thomas Ashley-Farrand's Healing Mantras, by Thomas Ashley-Farrand (Sounds True, 2000). Mantras to bring different qualities into your life. Audio.

The Singing Cure, by Paul Newham (Sounds True, 1998). A course in theraupeutic singing. Audio.

Chanting, by Robert Gass (Broadway, 2000). How to use the ancient power of chanting.

Music:

Enchanted: The Best of Robert Gass and On Wings of Song, Travelling the Sacred Sound Current: Divine Chants and Sacred Tones for Healing and Meditation by Crystal Voices and Deborah Van Dyke, *Medicine Buddha* by Jonathan Goldman, *Live on Earth* and *Breath of the Heart* by Krisna Das, *Shiva Stations* by Jai Uttal, *Healing Mantras* by Shri Anandi Ma and Dileepji Pathak, *Matriarch* by Joanne Shenandoah

Websites:

Sounds True
http://www.soundstrue.com

Healing Music Organization
http://www.healingmusic.org

Lady Slipper—approximately 15,000 (and growing!) current and past artists and titles
http://www.ladyslipper.org

New Age Music
http://www.newagemusic.com

Serenity Music
http://www.serenitymusic.com

National Public Radio—music heard on NPR
http://www.npr.org/music/index.html?loc=homebutton

SPIRIT SUCCOR

What Is It?

Within each and every one of us lies a source of wisdom, also known as our Spirit. We all need regular contact with this aspect of ourselves, and we often crave this contact, sometimes without knowing it. Regardless of our religious beliefs or disbeliefs, we must nurture this mysterious and often buried Spirit if we are to be fully alive and to experience peace. To neglect spiritual nurture is to pull the rug out from under all our efforts. It sometimes may not be as easy as nurturing other aspects of ourselves, but to nurture our Spirit is essential.

You'll Need:

Your imagination.

A quiet place to relax.

Music that inspires you to relax and go inside yourself.

When to Do It:

- When you feel a lack in your life but are not sure what to do.
- When you feel dulled by your present spiritual practices.
- When you need to touch the divine in life.

What to Do:

Peace Meditation

Relax. Close your eyes. Inhale and exhale gently. Focus on your breath going in, coming out. Now focus your closed eyes on the center of your forehead. Don't strain. Remember to breathe. Inhaling and exhaling, repeat silently to yourself, "I am at the center of peace. All is well in my world." Repeat this again and again while breathing deeply and maintaining your awareness on your forehead area.

Peace meditation
Spirit time
Spiritual nurturing with others
Journey-to-your-center meditation
Be a mythologist
Make a shrine

Spirit Time

Set aside a regular weekly time to nurture your spirit. It doesn't have to be on Sunday. A half hour is often sufficient. During your weekly time, you can:

See "Nature's Solace" for nature-oriented spiritual ideas.

Visit established places of worship. Try a different church every Sunday. Pay attention to the music, the architecture, the difference in the sermons. If this is not comforting, consider visiting a church or other spiritual site when it is empty and meditating there alone. Having an established place and time to go within is tremendously nurturing.

Read a spiritually satisfying book, or pursue a course of spiritual study. Try *Zen Mind, Beginner's Mind* or Louise Hay's books or read Joseph Campbell or study ancient Goddess civilizations.

Write a poem or story to or about your Spirit.

Write a prayer that celebrates your relationship to your Spirit or to your Higher Power.

See "Aesthetic Pleasures."

Study an aesthetic discipline.

See "Touch: Touch Walk"; "Body Delights: Feel Your Exercise"; or "Nutritional Music: A Sound Bath" for related activities.

Recognize and celebrate the spiritual component in an activity that you enjoy. Whether it is listening to a symphony or going for a silent walk in a park or running early in the morning, allow the experience to nurture your spirit. Prepare by meditating for a few moments. Keep your focus on the experience as it unfolds. Immerse yourself in the music or observe the dew or focus on your breath as you glide along. Spend some time afterward reflecting or writing in your journal about the experience.

See "Ease into Comforting Yourself" for an explanation of affirmations.

Work with affirmations related to your Spirit. Examples:

Deep at the center of my being, there is a well of perfect love.

I can now contact my inner Spirit.

I live completely in the here and now.

I am a divine being, put on earth to realize my divine purpose.

Spiritual Nurturing with Others

Plan a retreat. Try a wilderness challenge or an intriguing seminar. Or with like-minded friends travel to a place of spiritual significance, perhaps Greece to visit Goddess temples or Massachusetts to visit Walden Pond.

See "Nature's Solace: Plan a Transformational Wilderness Retreat" and "Women for Comfort: A Dream Wheel" for more ideas.

Attend a group meditation practice. To find one, check Zen, yoga, or Buddhist centers in your area, or ask your clergy person.

Find out about women's spirituality groups. Recent years have seen a tremendous explosion of interest in feminist spirituality. Look for notices in women's bookstores, check ads in the backs of women's magazines, ask your friends, or consider forming your own group. It can be as simple as a few women who get together to meditate, do journal exercises, and discuss spiritual questions.

See "Creating a Comfort Network: Strengthen Your Comfort Network" and "Women for Comfort."

Journey-to-Your-Center Meditation

Relax. Close your eyes. Inhale and exhale. Let your breath flow to every part of your body.

Imagine yourself walking in a beautiful and mysterious forest. You are not afraid, but relaxed and curious. Take in your surroundings as you stroll. Breathe deeply of the clean air.

You notice a large hole directly in front of you. You look down and see a staircase descending into the Earth. You intuitively know this staircase leads to the center of your self. You take a deep, deep breath and begin to descend.

You reach a landing. You rest, taking another deep breath. You continue until you reach another landing. Here you rest again and take a deep breath. Remind yourself you are safe and relaxed. As you descend toward your center, you take slower and deeper breaths.

You reach a hallway with a door marked in bold letters: THE CENTER OF MY SELF: There is nothing frightening inside. When you are ready, open the door and step inside.

Wander around. Observe your center. There may be a person or an animal here. Talk with them. Ask them, "What do I need to know in my life right now?" Or you may see a personal symbol or other important image. Take note of this. You may be given an object. Don't worry about understanding everything that is happening. Whatever you find, it is okay because it is you. Take plenty of time to explore.

When you are ready, walk back up the stairs, knowing you can return here any time you like. After a moment, you see the light at top of the stairs. It beckons you. Each step you take toward the light, you feel more alert and suffused with energy. When you reach the light, open your eyes. You are back in your room, safe, alert, and filled with knowledge of your Spirit Self.

See "Comfort Journal" for help.

Make your journey complete by creating a collage, image, sculpture, or story that expresses and honors what you have learned about your center. Try not to think too much while you do this, but instead let your unconscious mind speak through the materials of your choice. When you are finished, reflect on what you produced. Are there any insights or ideas you can integrate into your life?

Repeat this meditation often. New knowledge can always be found at our centers. We may go there to find answers, to be comforted, to center ourselves in a deep and satisfying way.

Be a Mythologist

Rollo May, along with many other writers and psychotherapists, believes our society needs a new and pertinent mythology if we are to find meaning in our lives. Our old myths are dead, and there are no new ones to fill the void. We especially lack a feminine mythology.

Remedy this by creating a personal myth.

You can write, paint, photograph, dance, or tell your myth as a story. Here are a few seed ideas to inspire you:

Reflect on a struggle in your life, and turn it into a positive, larger-than-life experience. An abortion, divorce, or the search for love can provide a starting point.

Use an important dream to begin your mythic journey.

Take a social problem, maybe the struggle between working and having children or the plight of homeless women, and bring it to a positive, mythic conclusion.

Write a fairy tale for your daughter (real or imaginary) about a heroine who uses her intelligence, power, and love to save the world.

Read Greek, Australian aboriginal, Native American, or Goddess myths for inspiration. Rewrite a myth you find, or personalize one that speaks to you.

Weave a story around a power object you possess, such as a special drum, scarf, picture, or bracelet.

You can create myths whenever you like. This is an excellent exercise to do when you are feeling disconnected from your family or ancestors. It is also helpful in specific problem solving, because in freeing your imagination to find mythic situations and solutions, you can brainstorm answers to your problems.

Make a Shrine

Whether in your personal sanctuary or on a bookshelf by your desk or on your bedside table, consider creating a personal shrine. In her book *Internal Affairs*, Kay Leigh Hagan talks about shrines as places where we can honor the things we hold sacred and precious. I think of a shrine as a personal spiritual site, a place where we can use objects and images to express ourselves. A shrine can also be a place where our playful self can interact with our spiritual self, and these interactions can teach and inform our conscious life.

Create your shrine any time you like. Create more than one. A lighted candle by a postcard of a place you want to visit is an idea. A gathering of

SPIRIT SUCCOR

See "A Personal Sanctuary" for more help.

objects that appeal to you, even if you're not sure why, is another. A book on meditation, a chime, and your meditation pillow are a possibility. Follow your impulses and experiment!

RESOURCES:

Life's Companion, by Christina Baldwin (Bantam, 1991). Spiritual journal exercises.

The Miracle of Mindfulness (Beacon, 1975), *Peace in Every Step* (Bantam, 1991), and *Present Moment, Wonderful Moment* (Parallax Press, 1990), all by Thich Nhat Hanh. Help seeing the spirit in everyday tasks.

Seven Masters, One Path: Meditation Secrets from the World's Greatest Teachers, by John Selby (HarperSanFrancisco, 2003). Selby brings together contemplative practices from seven revered spiritual masters to create a complete meditation program.

Essential Spirituality: The Seven Central Practices to Awaken Heart and Mind, by Roger Walsh (John Wiley and Sons, 2000). Common practices drawn from the world's major religions to create a guide to contemporary spirituality.

The Seeker's Guide, by Elizabeth Lesser (Villard, 2000). A personal journey and a wonderful selection of spiritual practices from one of the cofounders of Omega.

The Essential Rumi, by Coleman Barks (HarperSanFrancisco, 2004). The best translation of the mystic's crystal ravings.

When the Heart Waits: Spiritual Direction for Life's Sacred Questions, by Sue Monk Kidd (HarperSanFrancisco, 1992). A Christian exploration of how to enter deeply and fruitfully in times of transition and confusion. Also a memoir about midlife and spiritual crises.

In Sweet Company: Conversations with Extraordinary Women About Living a Spiritual Life, by Margaret Wolff (Margaret Wolff Unlimited, 2002). Participants include actress Olympia Dukakis, Sister Helen Prejean, Riane Eisler, Katherine Dunham, Grandmother Twylah Nitsch, Rabbi Laura Geller, Margaret Wheatley, and Dr. Lauren Artress.

Kosmic Consciousness, by Ken Wilber (Sounds True, 2004). A comprehensive and understandable introduction to a great thinker. Audio.

Websites:

Buddha Net
http://www.buddhanet.net

Belief Net
http://www.beliefnet.com

Omega
http://www.eomega.com

SOLITUDE

What Is It?

Solitude is choosing to spend time alone, briefly unaffected by others' wants and needs. It is the experience of being by yourself without feeling lonely.

Solitude is an essential self-nurturing activity. It helps us avoid fragmentation and burnout and encourages us to rebuild ourselves, to process our experiences. Solitude gives us the space to explore our creative selves and to confront our shadow side. Solitude is a requirement if we are to contact and learn from our Spirit.

Spending time with yourself is a skill that can be cultivated. And it is a skill well worth having and improving upon.

You'll Need:

To carve out time to be alone.

Private space.

Your journal, art supplies, and a pen.

A cardboard box.

When to Do It:

- When your soul is scattered all over creation.
- When you are saying, "Yes, I know it is important to take time for myself, but I just can't. I have too many responsibilities."
- When you are afraid to just sit still and be.

What to Do:

Take Responsibility

Repeat aloud, "How I choose to spend my time is my choice. I take full responsibility for my needs." Repeat this aloud every time you have an excuse for why you can't find time alone.

It is so easy to blame our lack of solitude on our children, our job, our partner. Take responsibility.

Take responsibility | *Creative notions*
Overcoming demons and guilt | *Silent solitude*
Structure | *The greatest gift*

Overcoming Demons and Guilt

It is impossible to know ourselves if we never take time to slow down and look inside. But we may be afraid to do so. We may be afraid we won't like what we find.

The only way to defeat your demons and face your guilt is to take the time alone to explore them, get to know them. What a catch-22! You feel afraid and guilty, so you don't create alone time, but without it, you'll never learn why you have these feelings!

Start with fifteen minutes of sitting alone in the backyard, on a balcony, or in a park. Be still. Look around. Watch life. Breathe deeply and slowly. Allow yourself to just be.

See "Courage Rituals" for help.

Structure

If you are afraid to spend time alone or if you are alone too much and want to be sure you have contact with others at some point in the day, it helps to provide a beginning and ending to your solitude.

If you are taking a day to be alone, make plans for dinner with a friend. If an entire day is too much, make lunch plans after a secluded morning.

Try creating a solitude ritual. You could acknowledge the beginning by playing a special piece of music and the end by eating Sunday dinner with your family.

See "Comfort Rituals."

Creative Notions

Free-associate in your journal with the words *seclusion*, *privacy*, *sacred time*, *solitude*.

With art supplies and a box, create a sculpture of your solitary time. On the inside of the box paste, draw, paint, or sculpt images that represent your solitary time. These images can be about plans, thoughts, actual events—whatever. On the outside, represent the blocks to your solitude. What competes for your time? What fears are stopping you? Represent any guilt or anger.

See "Body Delights: Whirling Dervish" for a starter idea.

Create a dance that expresses your seclusion.

List fifty things about your solitude—what you like about being alone and what you hate. Feel free to repeat items as many times as you like. Feel free to write entries that don't make logical sense. Try to keep your hand moving until you reach fifty.

Silent Solitude

Relax. Breathe slowly. Concentrate on the small moment of silence that exists between your inhalation and exhalation. If you are distracted by noises, focus on the silence between the noises. Imagine the silence underneath the ocean. Let this sense of immense solitude fill you. Stay with this as long as you like, then focus on the sounds around you again. Slowly open your eyes.

See "Nature's Solace: Prepare."

This is a great exercise to do in nature, high on a hill with the wind blowing through your hair, off in a corner of a garden, or by a body of water.

The Greatest Gift

Allow time for doing absolutely nothing. It may take practice, but the rewards are priceless.

RESOURCES:

The Woman's Retreat Book, by Jennifer Louden (HarperSanFrancisco, 1997). How to create your own retreat and embrace solitude in a new way.

A Year by the Sea: Thoughts of an Unfinished Woman, by Joan Anderson (Broadway, 2000). A memoir of solitude and self in the tradition of Sarton and Lindbergh.

LITTLE LOSSES

What Is It?

Life is filled with loss. This is inevitable. This chapter is about our little losses, the small disappointments and sad moments that invade our lives regularly: gaining weight instead of losing it, paying taxes, a fight with a friend.

Staying busy while ignoring your feelings blocks your emotional arteries and creates extra stress and depression. Dealing with your frustrations and pain as they come up can promote health, give you energy, and allow you to live in the moment.

You'll Need:

Private time.

Videotapes, books, whatever triggers grief for you.

When to Do It:

- After any event that makes you sad, regretful, or depressed, no matter how small.
- When you feel like you need a good cry.
- When you feel emotionally blocked and empty.

What to Do:

Grief Triggers

Letting your unpleasant emotions out is not encouraged in most cultures. You have probably been told at some point in your life not to cry, that crying is a sign of weakness. Because it may be difficult for you to cry and fully feel your sorrow, you might consider using a grief trigger. A grief trigger is anything that helps you experience your sad feelings, helps to get your feelings flowing. Emotional music and scenes from movies work best for me. Poetry and passages from favorite books are also possibilities. Sometimes you will need little help triggering your feelings. Different experiences require different things.

Spend a few days thinking and perhaps making notes about what moves you. What movies have struck a powerful chord in you? It might help to browse in a videotape store. Try

Grief triggers *A ritual for little losses*

remembering a movie in which the characters experience something similar to what you are feeling sad about. Try going to the library in search of books and tapes that might help trigger grief for you. Ask a trusted friend what movies or music or books make her sad.

A Ritual for Little Losses

Set aside time to slow down. Give yourself permission to cry, be sad, feel regret. Permission is the universal ingredient in dealing with little losses. If you feel like grieving, that is all that matters.

Begin this ritual by saying aloud, "I am upset about __________ , and I am now going to have a good cry." Or, if you aren't sure why you're feeling down, try, "I am feeling sad and blocked. I am going to explore this." You can also begin by asking yourself, "What could I be grieving for?"

See "A Personal Sanctuary."

It is almost always a good idea to do this work alone. If you need a stereo, Walkman, or VCR for your grief trigger, have it ready. Set up a space in which you feel private and safe.

See "Bathing Pleasures."

Taking a hot bath beforehand can help you relax. You could also consider doing this ritual in the bath.

Dress in especially comforting clothing.

Relax. Imagine your left hand holds all of your loss. Spend some time remembering the feelings and events surrounding this loss. Tense your left hand. Imagine yourself taking all the heartache and frustration surrounding this loss and concentrating it in your left hand. Squeeze hard.

Now concentrate on your right hand. Relax it. Imagine this hand holds total release, peace, and acceptance. Take a minute to feel these pleasant feelings. Feel them flow into your limp right hand.

Without moving too much or talking, begin to watch, read, or listen to your grief trigger. (If you don't need one, skip to the next paragraph.) Try playing or reading it over and over again. For example, you could read a poem that moves you a few times or program your stereo to play several sad songs over and over. You could also link together several sad scenes from movies, queuing the tapes to the appropriate spot and then playing them one after another. Repetition works wonders.

When your sad feelings are truly flowing, turn off the TV or stereo or put down the book.

Now clench your left hand again and consciously remind yourself of your loss, no matter how small or ill defined. Close your eyes. Clench your left hand as hard as you can. Let your sad feelings fill your heart. Allow yourself to wallow in your feelings. Wail, cry, gnash your teeth, chant, tone—whatever feels right.

See "Soothing Sounds: Chanting" and "Soothing Sounds: Toning."

When you have grieved enough, raise your relaxed right hand and your tense left hand until they are facing each other. Imagine that you are holding a large balloon between your hands. *Very slowly* try to press your hands together. Feel the pressure of the balloon as you squeeze. The balloon is the only thing between you and resolution, between you and feeling better. Your right hand is full of forgiveness, self-love, and release. Your left hand is heavy with frustration, sorrow, and nagging distress. If you can just bring your hands together, you will feel great. But the balloon is in the way. You can't quite get them together. . . . Keep trying. . . . The pressure builds. . . . SQUEEZE! Suddenly, the balloon *pops* and your hands clasp together, connecting in a shock of powerful, peaceful release. Breathe deeply. With each breath, send this wonderful, warm, relaxed sensation throughout your entire body.

To end your ritual, open your eyes and say, "I am cleansed and renewed."

A bath, a brisk walk, or even dancing to joyful music could feel good now.

RESOURCE:

Necessary Losses, by Judith Viorst (Fawcett, 1986). Best-selling book that explores the stages of our lives and the losses that go with them.

LETTING OFF STEAM

What Is It?

You know that feeling of total, blinding, teeth-grinding frustration, when everything is going wrong and you are brimming with anger, fed up with life, and all you want to do is tear someone's head off? What you need is to let off some steam.

Like a good cry or a belly laugh, setting aside time to let ourselves have a hot and angry outburst provides a wonderful catharsis, leaving us feeling "brushed clean" and free of our emotional baggage (at least for a while).

You'll Need:

Anger tools: Encounter bats or blockers (thickly padded sticks, found at sporting goods or martial arts supply stores) or a tennis racket wrapped with a towel.

A private space with a bed you can safely pound.

Paper and a pen.

A timer.

When to Do It:

- When someone cuts you off in traffic and you find yourself clenching your teeth and wanting to ram your car into theirs.
- When you misplace your keys and, while searching, hear someone screaming and realize it's you.
- When you find yourself in a bad mood and can't figure out a reason for it.

What to Do:

Some Facts About Anger

Anger is neither right nor wrong. It just is. We all get angry.

Don't worry about who is right or wrong. Anger has nothing to do with justice. You have to let yourself be angry before you can figure out how to fix the problem.

"Nice girls" do get angry. If they don't, they end up seriously depressed or sick or manipulative.

There is plenty to get angry about. Give yourself permission to feel. This isn't the Victorian era. You won't be locked up as a madwoman because you get mad.

Let It Flow

Set aside some time during which you won't be disturbed. Go to your private room where you can make as much noise as you need to. Place your anger tool on the nearby bed or couch.

Close your eyes. Let the power of your anger invade you, stir you up. If you need help feeling angry, picture a scene from your past in which you felt rage. Let that wild and disturbing emotion flow from your mind's eye into your arm and down to your hands. Keep playing angry scenes in your mind until you feel like you will pop.

Stomp over to the bed. Grab your anger tool with both hands. Sink to your knees. Close your eyes. Hold your anger tool over your head, arching back as far as you can. Take a deep breath and bring it forward, slamming the bed with all your might. Exhale sharply with each impact. Exaggerate your movements. Put all the force into it you can muster, even if you feel silly.

Each time you punch, loudly proclaim what you are angry at. "I'm outraged at my boss!" "I'm full of rage at myself for spending too much for that car!" "I'm angry at my mother for ruining Christmas!" "I'm furious at the poverty women are living in!" If you can't think of anything specific, repeat, "I am angry. I am angry!"

Keep going. Raise your voice. When you can't think of another item, repeat "I am angry" over and over again. Exhale. Use your entire body to pound the bed.

You will naturally bring your anger to a conclusion. You might end up screaming and beating the bed with your fists. That's great. When you feel ready, make one last HUGE arc and punch the bed while sighing or screaming loudly.

It is important to plan a transitional activity for after this exercise. You may feel emotionally raw, sensitive, or exhausted. You may be full of energy. Experiment with different activities that feel good. Perhaps taking a brisk walk or drawing in your journal will suit you. Or write a letter to your senator. Give yourself time to calm down.

If this exercise seems too contrived to work for you, try adapting it to an activity that feels more natural, like hitting tennis balls against a wall or kneading bread or raking leaves. Do try to maintain the structure of the ritual, and allow yourself to yell aloud. The act of physically expressing your anger and also giving a voice to it is the core of this exercise.

Unsent Letters

Write a letter that says absolutely everything you have ever wanted to say. Address your letter to whatever or whomever you are angry at: a person (Dear Sonja), an institution (Dear United States Government), an event or holiday (Dear Birthday). You can also address the letter to someone who would understand your feelings: a therapist, a teacher, a spiritual figure, your Spirit. Or you don't have to address it to anyone.

Next time you are feeling angry or tense, get your paper and pen. Find a place where you won't be disturbed. Set your timer for twenty minutes. Put the pen to paper, and start writing. Don't stop writing until the timer goes off. Pour everything out. Don't hold anything back. Don't censor yourself. No one is ever going to read this letter.

See "Nutritional Music: Intensifying Your Mood" for another letting-off-steam exercise.

When your twenty minutes are up, burn the letter, and envision your anger going up in smoke. Scatter the ashes in an appropriate place. While doing so, imagine yourself scattering your anger, frustration, and pain away.

RESOURCES:

The Dance of Anger, by Harriet Goldhor Lerner, Ph.D. (Quill, 1997). A guide to using anger as a constructive force.

Feeling Good: The New Mood Therapy, by David D. Burns, M.D. (Avon, 1999). One of the best books written on coping with depression. Great section on anger.

Loving What Is, by Katie Byron with Stephen Mitchell (Harmony Books, 2002). Learn how to use a process called "The Work" to transform negative feelings into a new reality.

Toxic People: Ten Ways of Dealing with People Who Make Your Life Miserable, by Lillian Glass (St. Martin's Press, 1997). Learn thirty different "toxic" personality types and how to deal more effectively with them, as well as identify your own toxic behavior patterns.

The Marriage of Spirit: Enlightened Living in Today's World, by Leslie Temple-Thurston with Brad Laughlin (Core Light Publications, 2000). Blends mystical thinking with mentally oriented Western thinking to assist the reader in living a life more in tune with their divine nature. Great section and exercises on judgments.

A Meditation to Help With Anger and Forgiveness, by Belleruth Naparstek (Image Paths, 2002). Another amazing imagery tape and affirmations from the queen of imagery.

A FORGIVENESS RITUAL

What Is It?

Forgiveness is powerful stuff. We all have been hurt, and we all have hurt others. Our lives are littered with should haves, could haves, and if onlys. This emotional garbage plugs our hearts and minds and makes us very uncomfortable. Anxiety and guilt plague us.

By practicing a simple ritual, we can get the juices of our spirit flowing again. We can unblock potent energy. As a regular spiritual practice, forgiveness helps us to be more loving, flexible, and understanding.

You'll Need:

Your imagination.

A body of water. A calm ocean, a lake, or a wilderness pond is ideal. However, a swimming pool or bathtub works fine.

When to Do It:

- When you are harboring resentment toward a friend or lover even after you have talked it out.
- When you often find yourself saying things like, "I wish I'd done that," or "If only I would have. . . ."
- When you can't forgive yourself for a mistake, mishap, or painful event.

What to Do:

Forgiveness Baptism

Decide on a time on or near the full moon when you can privately visit a body of water or a swimming pool. You can also do this as a visualization, without water.

Begin by focusing on your breath. Feel how easily it glides in and out of your body. Imagine your breath moving throughout your body, easing every area of tension it encounters. Breathing deeply, walk slowly toward the water. Stop to gaze up at the moon. Feel the calm energy of the moonlight finding its way deep into your soul. The moonlight and your slow, deep breaths mingle and relax your body completely.

You reach the water. The moonlight gives the water magical powers tonight. Disrobe and slip

Forgiveness baptism

in. Cup your hands together, fill them with water, and pour the water on yourself. With each touch of the magic water, say, "I forgive myself." "I forgive myself for (fill in what you need to forgive yourself for: hurting someone you love, a mistake, regrets). I am now releasing my remorse and sorrow. I forgive myself."

After you have forgiven yourself for everything you can remember, visualize someone who has hurt you. Splash water at this image, saying, "I forgive you." Imagine others who have hurt you. Release them by anointing their images with water too.

When you are finished, glide underwater. As the magic water closes over your head, say to yourself, "I am now cleansed. I am free."

Walk out of the water and dress. Take a moment to gaze at the moon and to be thankful for your new peace. Breathing deeply, return the way you came.

RESOURCES:

Woulda, Coulda, Shoulda, by Dr. Arthur Freeman, Ph.D., and Rose DeWolf (Perennial, 1992). Uses cognitive therapy techniques to help you get over past mistakes.

Forgiveness and Other Acts of Love, by Stephanie Dowrick (W. W. Norton, 1997). Bringing compassion, appreciation, and insight into your life when you need it most.

Forgiveness Is a Choice: A Step-by-Step Process for Resolving Anger and Restoring Hope, by Robert D. Enright (American Psychological Association, 2001). The definitive, well-researched, truly effective guide to healthy forgiveness.

The Art of Forgiveness, Lovingkindness, and Peace, by Jack Kornfield (Bantam, 2002). A collection of age-old teachings, modern stories, and time-honored practices for bringing healing, peace, and compassion into your daily life.

See "Creative Selfishness: Dealing with Guilt" for more help.

THE SHADOW SIDE OF COMFORT

What Is It?

Many of us believe that if we take the time to comfort ourselves, we may never do a lick of work again. Instead, we will lounge on a chaise eating bonbons. (What are bonbons anyway?) So isn't saying there is a shadow side of comfort the same as admitting self-nurture is dangerous and we would be better off doing another load of laundry?

No! Just because there is a shadow aspect of comfort doesn't mean comfort is bad. It does mean that it is possible to use comfort and being comfortable as excuses to limit or negate ourselves. We may stay put in a less-than-great relationship because it is comfortable. We may not go to night school because it would make us uncomfortable. We may spend our weekends doing boring activities because this is comforting. You can recognize and work to transform this facet of comfort, but please don't use it as a reason to stop nurturing yourself.

Why do we sometimes allow comfort to limit our potential? Why do we sometimes comfort ourselves in not-so-great ways? To avoid responsibility, to hide in self-delusion, to remain self-righteous and safe from failure, and to avoid fear or anxiety are possibilities. (These are just possibilities. No blame.)

But although comfort does contain a "dark" side, as we each contain a shadow self, this aspect of comfort can be transformed into stimulating and rich self-nurturing if we are willing to experience a little discomfort first. The transformation can be brought about by being mindful, by paying attention to how you are nurturing yourself and what effects this nurturing is having on your life.

You'll Need:

Your journal and a pen.

When to Do It:

- When you reward yourself for achievements in ways that leave you feeling rotten or stale afterward.

Mindful comfort
Unmindful comfort
Self-defeating rewards
Overcoming procrastination
Comfort as avoidance

- When there is something you've been wanting to accomplish for a long time but never got around to doing.
- When you use comfort to shut off or stuff down feelings of anger, frustration, sadness, or any other vital emotions.
- When you use comfort as a replacement for building intimate relationships with others.

What to Do:

Mindful Comfort

If you take the time to stop and be aware of how you feel when comforting yourself, you begin a chain reaction that can lead to many places. For instance, when I started paying attention to how I comforted myself, I realized that staying home weekend nights and ordering Thai food and watching videos was comforting and safe, but it also could be limiting and boring. It made me uncomfortable at first, but I found when I made unusual plans for the weekend, I almost always came away stimulated and enriched. On a more profound level, practicing mindful comfort might help you leave a boring job, finish the novel that has lain in your drawer for five years, or travel around the world.

Try this: Next time you need to comfort yourself, stop, close your eyes, and ask, "Is this really what I want right now?" If the answer is yes, wonderful, full speed ahead. If you aren't sure, go ahead anyway, but check in with yourself a couple of times to see if what you chose is satisfying you and truly making you feel better.

See "When I Think of Comfort, I Think of Food: Truly Comfort Yourself"; "Money, Money, Money: Inherit from Your Intuition"; and "Simplify: Three Good Questions" for more help activating your inner voice.

Unmindful Comfort

Sometimes unmindful comfort is the only kind that will do the job. There are Friday nights when I must have Thai food and *The Little Mermaid.* I need to shut down, tune out. Mindful implies observing yourself, and always observing yourself is not comforting. A balance is needed. If you can learn (through experimentation and regularly asking, "Is this

See "Courage Rituals."

really what I want right now?") what is truly nurturing to you, you can achieve a balance between conscious comforting and forget-about-everything comfort. It takes trial and error and a bit of courage.

Self-Defeating Rewards

How do you treat yourself for a job well done? Do you sometimes reward yourself in a self-defeating way instead of a nurturing way? Examples include having a few drinks after a good day at work only to find you are fuzzy and tired the next morning. Or going shopping and spending too much money, then feeling guilty and not enjoying your purchases. Or throwing a party when you would rather be alone.

Entrenched patterns from our childhood, pressure from friends or colleagues, and a deeply held belief that we don't deserve this good fortune, coupled with a lack of awareness, often lead us to comfort ourselves in an empty or self-abnegating style.

The simple awareness test works well here too. Next time you have something to celebrate, take a minute before you do anything and ask yourself, "How do I want this reward to make me feel? What do I truly want to reward myself with?" Let's say you receive word of a big promotion. Your first thought is to go to the mall after work and shop, perhaps buy that pair of shoes you've had your eyes on. But first, you retreat to a quiet spot, close your eyes, and ask yourself the magic questions. If nothing else comes to your mind, you can still reward yourself by shopping. But perhaps, after asking yourself these magic questions, an image appears on the screen of your mind's eye. It is you walking alone on the beach at sunset, then going home to write in your journal and call a close friend. You get a good feeling from this image and decide this would be a better reward than shopping.

By the simple act of checking and choosing, we send a healthy message to ourselves: Our opinions and needs are valued; therefore we are worthwhile. People who feel they are worthwhile are the most honestly comfortable, successful, and happy people around.

Overcoming Procrastination

Sometimes the most self-nurturing thing we can do for ourselves is to do what we've been putting off. The comfort comes not in the facing and doing, but in the glow of satisfaction that follows.

But please don't trick yourself into believing that you can never do anything frivolous or pleasurable because you sometimes use comfort to avoid a problem. Many times avoidance is necessary because your heart and mind need to gather strength before they can tackle the issue or work at hand. Please don't use this section as an excuse to beat yourself up. There is a fine line here, and only you can know when you need to take action and when you need to pull back.

Try these ideas for overcoming blocks to getting things done:

Break your task down into small, concrete steps. If you need to finish painting the bedroom, make a list of everything you need for the job and every step it takes to get it done. Do one item on the list right now.

Ask for help. You can barter with a neighbor for help designing your business cards. You can get friends together and brainstorm solutions. You can trade with a friend: spend one Saturday tackling all the little guilt details in your life and the next Saturday doing hers.

See "Money, Money, Money: Barter Leverage" and "Creating a Comfort Network."

Dress the part. If you hate to do yard work, buy a big straw hat and flowered gloves to wear. If you loathe exercise, buy some truly wild leotards and socks.

Make it fun. If you hate to clean, play the B-52s' "Housework" cut from their album *Bouncing off the Satellites*. If you detest going to the doctor, sandwich the visit between two comfort events, like browsing in a children's bookstore and walking on the beach.

See "Reading like a Child" and "Nature's Solace."

Make it easy to do repetitive tasks that you hate. Create a convenient and well-organized place to pay your bills. Keep your dental floss on top of the TV. Place a watering can near your houseplants. Make the time to take the frustration out of these already unpleasant tasks.

Comfort as Avoidance

At times we use comfort as an excuse to avoid emotional closeness in our lives. We may nap instead of reaching out to friends when we're hurting. We may watch lots of TV instead of talking to our partners about a behavior of theirs that made us deeply angry. We may shop instead of dealing with our fears about money.

To identify when you are using comfort as a way to avoid an emotional issue, watch for feelings of guilt or unease around comforting activities; notice if you choose to comfort yourself in repetitious ways; see if self-nurturing activities that once made you feel good now leave you feeling dull or unhappy; notice if you are using comfort solely to tune out or shut down; glance at the sections "Little Losses" and "Letting off Steam," and observe yourself to see if these exercises scare you or make you anxious.

If you get a sense that you are using comfort to avoid a problem, grab your journal and write down the question "What am I avoiding?" Shut your eyes for a moment, and just let the answer float out. As soon as it does, write it down. If nothing comes to mind, **relax** and ask yourself again. If nothing comes, close your journal and ask yourself again in a few days. Sometimes we are not ready to deal with the answer, so don't force it.

When you get an answer, the next step is to answer the question "What am I getting out of avoiding ____________?" (Fill in the blank.) Close your eyes, and reflect on that one as well. Again, when you feel ready, write down everything that comes to mind, no matter how fragmentary or weird.

Wait a few days. Reread the answers to the questions. Set a timer for fifteen minutes, and write down every solution you can think of to this problem. (The timer creates pressure and helps your mind work better.) Again, don't censor yourself. Reflect on your answers. Identify the first step in solving your problem. Perhaps it is interviewing therapists. Perhaps it is making one new friend. Perhaps it is setting aside an hour to talk with your partner or lover.

See "Creating a Comfort Network" and "Comforting Communication."

Remind yourself with your nurturing voice that things can get better, then take one small step toward solving your problem right now. Comfort yourself afterward in an especially warm and wonderful way.

See "Your Nurturing Voice."

RESOURCES:

Owning Your Own Shadow: Understanding the Dark Side of the Psyche, by Robert A. Johnson (HarperSanFrancisco, 1991). Help working with your shadow self.

Journal to the Self: Twenty-two Paths to Personal Growth, by Kathleen Adams (Warner Books, 1990). Adams, a psychotherapist, provides several ways to utilize a journal to achieve personal growth, express creativity, and enhance quality of life through journaling.

Embracing Your Inner Critic: Turning Self-Criticism into a Creative Asset, by Hal and Sidra Stone (HarperSanFrancisco, 1993). Drs. Hal and Sidra Stone are the creators of the "Voice Dialogue" therapeutic process, which gives voice to the different personality attributes we all have living inside us. In this book, they show how to use your inner critic as a helpful ally, rather than a despised enemy.

Stretching Lessons: The Daring That Starts from Within, by Sue Bender (HarperCollins, 2001). Learn how to listen to your own voice and have faith and trust in what you are feeling and to enjoy the unfolding of your life's story.

There Must Be More Than This, by Judith Wright (Broadway, 2003). Wright develops some wonderful ideas around shadow comforts, which she calls "soft addictions."

The Sedona Method: Your Key to Lasting Happiness, Success, Peace, and Emotional Well-Being, by Hale Dwoskin (Sedona Press, 2003). A Western approach to Buddhist philosophy for changing damaging thought patterns.

Website:

There Must Be More
http://www.theremustbemore.com

CHALLENGE COMFORT

What Is It?

To stretch ourselves is to be excited, to awaken, to see life opening before us. When we stretch our comfort zones by traveling alone, when we expand our minds by reading philosophy, when we expose ourselves to failure by learning something new, we whet our appetite for life and bless ourselves with exhilarating self-care at the same time.

You'll Need:

Courage.

Stimulating activities.

Demanding books.

Fascinating people to converse with.

When to Do It:

- When your life feels gray and dull.
- When you can't remember the last time something exciting took your breath away.
- When you can't remember the last time you had to dig deep within yourself to meet a challenge.

What to Do:

Expand Your Comfort Zone

You define your personal comfort zone every day. You might be comfortable attending a movie alone during the week but not on the weekend. You might ask for a seven thousand-dollar raise, but nine thousand seems impossible.

Spend a few days or a week in loving observation of your comfort zone. Get an idea of what your limits are. Clues to look for in the process of learning about your limits include stopping yourself from trying something and then regretting it; saying things like, "I would never do that," or "I can't do that," or "Maybe someday"; and feeling guilty about enjoying yourself.

Start to expand yourself by doing something small that currently makes you uncomfortable.

Hate eating out alone? Try having lunch at a familiar restaurant. Afraid of telling a friend who talks too long on the phone that you need to get off? Practice firmly but kindly saying, "I can't talk anymore. I have to go. I'm hanging up now." Every other day or so, or once a week, push yourself gently to do something a little more challenging.

Try to stay tuned in to your feelings while testing your limits. Fear and anxiety are normal. You will mostly feel them before you take action. Taking the action is actually a relief.

As you move on to bigger challenges, take some time beforehand to imagine the worst happening. Imagine everything that could happen if you failed. Get into the details. Make sure you imagine the very worst. When I gave my first workshop, I imagined everyone hating it and walking out in the middle. Take a few minutes to wallow in your embarrassment or anguish, then acknowledge to yourself that this is the worst that can happen. Get your mind around it. Accept this. You can stop worrying now because you've conquered the unknown.

Remember, when expanding your horizons, *do not berate yourself. Go at your own pace.* Don't compare yourself to women who climb mountains or mothers with ten children. Don't compare yourself to anyone. This is difficult, but try.

The experience of expanding your comfort zone is one of empowerment. You become more confident, flexible, more able to deal with the ups and downs of life, and more capable of choosing the kind of life you want.

Learn Something New

As adults, we can become too rigid in our mental outlooks and patterns, and this can make it difficult for us to learn new things. Our egos get in the way and we automatically want to be able to do it and do it right the first time. It is quite a challenge to quiet our egos and expose ourselves to learning. If we can leave behind our mind's chatter, we win the possibility of expanding our inner selves. It helps to:

Choose a nonthreatening environment. Instead of enrolling in college to learn oil painting, take a class at a community center. Find friends who want to play tennis more than win tennis. Barter with an acquaintance for carpentry lessons.

Seek out good teachers. Teachers should teach us how to learn. They should be supportive, not punitive. Insist on kind teaching. You deserve it.

"Seek the how," as the Sufis say. Immerse yourself in the process; open yourself to the challenge, not the end result. Study or learn something for the sake of doing it, without caring whether you are good at it or talented or going somewhere. Forget the end result.

If you are worried about challenging yourself, take a piece of paper and let your critical voice have her say. Set a timer for fifteen minutes, tell her she has your uninterrupted attention, and let her rip.

Expect to feel awkward, unsure, unskilled. Expect yourself to make mistakes. If you can get away from yourself long enough to fail, you will open doors to exciting places, both inside and outside of yourself.

Deal with Failure

Failure is implicit in challenge. It wouldn't be a challenge if we knew we could do it. Nonetheless, it is far from comforting to flop. If this happens, how can it be made less awful?

See "Your Nurturing Voice."

Don't beat yourself up.

See "Comfort Rituals: Letter to Yourself" for a variation.

Write a love letter to yourself. Pour all the love you can muster into this note of self-acceptance. Mail and read it when it arrives.

Make a list of fifty things you learned from whatever you failed at. Please, don't stop writing until you come up with the fifty, even if you have to repeat two items twenty-five times.

Remember ten other times you failed and survived.

Lick your wounds by retreating from the world.

See "Hiding Under the Covers."

Prepare some insurance for failure blues by writing and hiding a few comfort cards. Also, warn a close friend you are stretching your wings and may need to be scraped up off the pavement once or twice before you get the hang of flying.

See "Comfort Cards" and "Comforting Communication: Be Direct."

Some Challenging Ideas

See "Courage Rituals: Courage Ritual with Friends"; "Creating a Comfort Network"; "Women for Comfort: Trips for and by Women"; "Nature's Solace: Plan a Transformational Wilderness Retreat"; "Aesthetic Pleasures: Make Beauty"; "The Power of Goals"; and "Nurture Others" for more challenging comfort ideas.

Write a poem. Read something difficult in an area you have never explored, like physics or Zen philosophy. Write down your moral code. Define your life's purpose. Work at a hospice for the dying. Admit you were wrong to someone you love. At a party, introduce yourself to someone who looks interesting. Wander around a park without a plan. Take a ride in a hot-air balloon. Canoe the Amazon. Sew a shirt. Fix the plumbing. Trust your intuition. Tell someone you love them.

RESOURCES:

Have It All: Body, Mind, Heart, and Spirit Together Again at Last, by Phil Porter (Wing It Press, 1997). Playful ideas for embodying wholeness.

The Art of Possibility: Transforming Professional and Personal Life, by Rosamund Stone Zander and Benjamin Zander (Penguin, 2002). A mind-expanding look at how the stories we tell ourselves shape our choices.

The Path of Least Resistance, by Robert Fritz (Fawcett Books, 1989). Fritz is not a great writer, but his ideas on how to create work!

Keys to Your Highest Potential, by Martha Howard, M.D. A powerful combo of hypnosis, imagery, and affirmations to remove self-imposed blocks to success. Audio.

Websites:

Enlightenment
http://www.enlightenment.com

Spirituality and Health
http://www.spiritualityhealth.com

Naked Integral
http://www.integralnaked.org

THE POWER OF GOALS

What Is It?

Fulfilling your heart's desire is a very nurturing experience. Goals present a powerful way to help us achieve what we most desire in life, but they can also become dangerous prisons that keep our eyes fastened on our destinations instead of being open to the journey unfolding around us. It is crucial to set goals that are truly ours (not our family's or our lover's or our friend's) and to know when to let go of goals that are no longer working for us. It is magical to strive for and reach a goal. It is equally magical to know when to change course.

You'll Need:

Your journal and a pen.

When to Do It:

- When your life lacks focus.
- When your present goals seem stale or false.
- When you would like to change careers or find your life's purpose.
- When there is something you want to achieve and guidelines would help.

What to Do:

These ideas were inspired by the work of Barbara Sher, author of *Wishcraft*, and Shakti Gawain, workshop leader and author of *Creative Visualization*.

Your Ideal Day

To get what you want, you must know what you want—not what you *should* want. Forget your mother, your bank account, your fears of growing old alone and broke. You can consider those elements later. During this exercise, consider only what your heart's desire is. Remember, it is you that must be satisfied.

Place your comfort journal close by. **Relax.** Begin to imagine your ideal day. Start in the morning, and visualize your entire day.

Where do you wake up? In a plush hotel room, in your mansion in Palm Beach, in a shack on a South Sea isle? What do you do all day? Trade commodities, write best-sellers, teach little children, create sculpture, work as a golf pro? What is your ideal working environment? Do you live alone? What kind of people populate your ideal day? What do you do after work? Do you even choose work? Forget reality. Let your imagination flow and provide you with as many details as possible. When you are ready, open your eyes and record your ideal day in your journal.

Goals

Goals need to be specific. "To be famous" is not as good as "I'll be famous when I star in my own TV show." For a goal to function satisfactorily, you must be able to know when you have achieved it. Otherwise no end is in sight, which makes it hard to get started and impossible to finish.

Take a blank piece of paper, and write *Career* across the top. Reread your ideal day. Now, list all the specific career goals you can derive from your ideal day. Don't worry how wacky they are. Write everything down.

Next, write why you want to achieve these things. Because you want spiritual fulfillment, money, peace on Earth? Be honest. Also, note how you will feel when you achieve your goal. Important, satisfied, at peace?

Do the same for other areas: relationships (with yourself, family, mate, lover, coworkers); self-care; fun (travel, leisure, whatever interests you included in your ideal day); lifestyle (what kind of environment you live in, how you dress, what your house or apartment looks like), and inner life (spiritual goals, personal growth). Use a separate sheet for each area.

Break Down

Pick one area, and reread your list of goals. Choose the one you would most like to achieve in the next five years. Write this goal in the form of an affirmation. "I now live in a beautiful ranch house on one hundred acres of land in northern New Mexico." Be descriptive, but keep it simple. Be sure to write your goal in the present tense.

Now break that five-year goal down into one-year intervals. If you want to have a house and land in five years, your one-year goal might be getting a raise.

Take it down to six months. Your six-month goal could be to save one-thousand dollars.

Now decide on your one-month goal. This might be to find out what land costs in New Mexico and to read a book about investing.

Finally, set a related goal for this week. You might want to visualize your ideal day taking place in your ranch house.

It is okay to have more than one small goal as you break it down. Just don't overburden yourself, or you'll be so overwhelmed you'll chuck the whole plan.

Repeat this process for the remaining areas: relationships, self-care, fun, lifestyle, and inner life. (You don't have to. You can stick with one set of goals. Keep this fun; try not to turn it into work.)

Getting Off Track

We aim for the stars and find it takes a long time to reach them. We start to wonder if we actually want to go there. When that happens, check back to why you wanted to achieve your goal. Close your eyes and see yourself moving into your house in New Mexico. What does it feel like? If it still feels good, keep going. If it doesn't, it might be time to revise this desire.

What You Already Have

Check and see what elements of your ideal day are already in place. Your job? Your lover? Your house? Give yourself a big hug for what is good about your life already.

Nine Lives

Barbara Sher presents a beautiful plan for those of us who have more than one life goal. Maybe you want to be an executive and a painter? To travel and to have a child? You have several options. You can work toward fulfilling one goal and then switch to another. For example, spend five years being an executive and then five being a painter. Or you can live two lives at once. Be an executive during the week and a painter on weekends and holidays. Or you can alternate in smaller blocks of time, say a year toward one life goal, then three months toward another. Adjust your goal plan to include what you need. It is all up to you.

Impossible Dreams

You want to be an Olympic star but you are forty-five and suffer from mild arthritis. You feel you can't physically achieve your goal. Well, you are probably right, but you can achieve the *feeling* behind the goal. What is it about being an Olympic star that you crave? The thrill of crossing the finish line while people cheer? The satisfaction of long hours of training paying off? The camaraderie of people working for a common cause together? Pinpoint the feeling behind your dream, and then you can find a concrete way to achieve it. Sample a few activities to help you get a taste of what you crave. Take part in a walkathon for your favorite charity. Train and run in a five-kilometer race. Volunteer to coach your local special Olympics. There is more than one way to catch a dream.

Change Is Good

Goals are made to be changed, molded, thrown away. A goal is not sculpted in stone but is fluidly written in happy sweat. For goal setting to be honestly self-nurturing, you must check with yourself often (once a month is good) to be sure you want what you are working for and that you are enjoying the process of getting there. Nothing is more depressing than working yourself to the bone for something, achieving it, and then realizing you didn't sincerely want it in the first place.

RESOURCES:

Wishcraft: How to Get What You Really Want, by Barbara Sher with Annie Gottlieb (Ballantine Books, 1979). Help fulfilling your life's dreams.

Ninety Days to a New Direction, by Laura Berman Fortgang (Jeremy Tarcher/Penguin, 2004). Fortgang is a personal coach, author, and mom of three. Try her amazing plan to move from being stuck to a new life—in just ninety days!

Excuse Me, Your Life Is Waiting, by Lynn Grabhorn (Hampton Roads Publishing, 2000). Learn how to use your thoughts and feelings as a way to create more of what you want in your life.

Goal Setting 101, by Gary Ryan Blair (The Goals Guy, 2000). A little no-nonsense book that outlines goal setting and achieving in a straightforward, easy-to-follow way.

The Creative Fire Myths and Stories About the Cycles of Creativity, by Clarissa Pinkola Estes (Sounds True, 1993). A cassette series for people who are creators and also people who long to create but feel stuck by their own fears, blocks, and judgments.

NURTURE OTHERS

What Is It?

Reaching out nurtures our self-worth. Helping others makes us feel good. We grow to believe other people care about us, which is excellent comfort when we are depressed. Also, nurturing others teaches us humility and gratitude. Through caring for those in need, be they friends or strangers, we can touch the ultimate goodness of the world by touching the goodness in ourselves.

But remember, this is not an opportunity to burn yourself out. This is not an endorsement to put everyone else's needs in front of your own or to overcommit to a volunteer program or to get sucked into a needy friend's problems. Please, take care of yourself first, even in the act of taking care of others.

You'll Need:

Information on volunteer opportunities in your area.

Goodies for friends.

A little time, energy, and love.

When to Do It:

- When you need a break from your own problems.
- When you need to feel needed and part of the larger picture of life.
- When you are feeling depressed, overwhelmed, and discouraged about the state of the world.

What to Do:

Close By

If big, organized volunteer work overwhelms or scares you, start small. Hundreds of opportunities exist for nurturing the people around you.

Visit an elderly person on your block. Give ten dollars to a charity you've never helped before. Give a homeless person all your change, and look her in the eye when you do so. Open a door for a stranger. Pick up trash on your street. Learn the names of your neighbors.

Close by
Help people you know
A comfort bag
Volunteer to learn
Volunteer to change

Help People You Know

Mail your partner a love letter. Tuck a "you're a great kid" note in your children's lunch bag. Give a neighbor half of your casserole. Write a letter to a lonely aunt, uncle, or grandmother. Take a friend's children to the park to give your friend a rest.

See "Comfort Cards."

Clip a pertinent article to give to a coworker the next day. Information and resources are great gifts. Habitually share the name of that great inexpensive restaurant you discovered or the wonderful book you read on Sunday.

Surprise your partner, child, or friend with a little something they want: renting a movie they want to see, giving them a small gift certificate, baking them their favorite muffins.

A Comfort Bag

A delightful, personal way to reach out to a friend in need is to deliver a bag (or basket or box) filled with comforting goodies. The surprise of a gift during hard times can be invaluable. Tailor the bag to the recipient's current needs. Some ideas for the contents: chocolate kisses, a favorite inspirational book, scented soap or lotion, a small reminder to laugh (perhaps a miniature troll or a wind-up toy), slick magazines (great gift for a sick friend), a bottle or two of essential oils (try rose or lavender), a long-stemmed rose, fresh coffee beans, a split of champagne, a snapshot from a shared happy day, an appreciation letter (a note listing all their qualities you cherish and respect). The choices are endless.

Volunteer to Learn

Make a double whammy of loving yourself by helping others while cultivating your mind or exploring a new occupational interest. Become a docent at an art or natural history museum. Answer phones for a small art gallery. Be an usher for a symphony series.

Explore being an apprentice, on weekends or nights, to an artist or crafts person you admire. Volunteer at your public television or radio station during the pledge drive.

Train to be a counselor or hot line volunteer for a rape crisis or life transition center. Share your career expertise in your public school system. Teach something you're an expert in at a community center.

Volunteer to Change

Depressed about the environment, the political climate, women's rights? The quickest way to feel better is to pound the bed and scream.

See "Letting off Steam."

Slower but more lasting peace comes from action. Decide on one problem that angers or depresses you the most or that feels closest to your experience (women's issues, minority rights, local environmental concerns). Decide how much time you can commit, then research courses of action or brainstorm with friends to decide what to do. Don't overwhelm yourself. The quickest way to feel worse, and to quit, is to take on too much too soon.

Follow your inner voice, and don't play the martyr.

RESOURCES:

Your phone directory is a great resource for help finding places to volunteer. They list volunteer centers and other agencies for your area.

See "Women for Comfort: Support Women" and "Animal Antidotes: Animal Activism" for more helping ideas.

Your local newspaper may carry a section describing volunteer opportunities once a week or once a month. Clip the articles and file for future reference.

How to Make the World a Better Place: 116 Ways You Can, by Jeffery Hollender (Norton, 1995). Lots of excellent, doable ideas.

Make a Difference: America's Guide to Volunteering and Community Service, by Arthur I. Blaustein (John Wiley, 2003). Help deciding where your volunteer talents would be best applied.

Websites:

Volunteer Abroad
http://www.i-to-i.com

SIMPLIFY

What Is It?

Simplifying your life is a profound way to care for yourself. The feeling I get when I pare away unnecessary possessions, responsibilities, and desires in my life is akin to skinny-dipping in the cold, rough Pacific ocean: bracing, exhilarating, and a little scary.

To nurture ourselves by adopting a simpler lifestyle is to encounter a graceful and comforting place within ourselves and within the world.

You'll Need:

The courage to pare away what you no longer need.

When to Do It:

- When you life lacks balance.
- When you feel your lifestyle is preventing you from living.
- When you feel you're drowning under a sea of work responsibilities, social obligations, car repairs, and yard work.

What to Do:

Three Good Questions

Simplifying your life is simple but not easy. Decide what you want and must have, and let the rest go by the wayside. To help accomplish this pruning, here are three questions to ask when making decisions, setting goals, or planning your day.

Will this matter tomorrow?

Will this matter in ten years?

Will this matter at the end of my life?

Try to make these questions part of your regular thought patterns. Next time you are uptight about your job, ask yourself, will this matter in ten years? Sometimes the answer will be yes, usually no.

Three good questions *Perspective*
Priorities

Priorities

Each morning spend a few minutes deciding what matters most today. What do you need to do above all else? Focus on only one activity. Let the more trivial things in your life fall by the wayside if necessary. And don't cheat by always picking work or family. Remember self-nurturing activities too!

Perspective

Another useful tool in deciding what is important to you is perspective.

Try climbing to the top of a tall structure. Spend some time looking down.

Lie on the grass on a clear night. Study the vast expanse of stars above you.

See "Nurture Others."

Serve dinner at a shelter for homeless women. Learn about what their lives were like and are like now.

Sit by a large body of water.

Think back to a time in your life when your values were called into question, perhaps during an illness or when someone you loved died. What were your observations and resolutions at that time?

RESOURCES:

The Joy of Simple Living: Over 1,500 Simple Ways to Make Your Life Easy and Content—At Home and at Work, by Jeff Davidson (Rodale, 1999). So many simplify-your-life books are overly simplistic—not this one!

The Simple Living Guide, by Janet Luhrs (Broadway, 1997). A vast compilation of ideas. The Bible of simple living.

Websites:

Simple Living
http://www.simpleliving.com

Simple Living Network
http://www.simpleliving.net

REMINDING YOURSELF

What Is It?

You have experimented with some of the comforts in this book and have nurtured yourself on many different levels. But life is an ongoing process, and unless comfort is an ongoing part of your life, you become overwhelmed and stressed again. Don't forget about yourself. Don't forget that you are worth love and attention.

You'll Need:

A personal memento.

When to Do It:

- Daily.

What to Do:

Find a Token

To remind yourself how vital it is to nurture yourself, find a small token that is unique to you, something that will remind you to care for yourself when things get crazy.

Perhaps you picked up a smooth stone from a solitude walk on the beach. Or a lock of your beloved's hair. Or a toy you had as a child. Carry your token with you so you can be reminded to nurture yourself. Slip it in your pocket, wear it as a necklace, hang it from your rearview mirror. It helps to change tokens every now and then, otherwise they become stale and too familiar.

Funny Time

Remind yourself not to take life so seriously by making fun of time. Try wearing a silly watch. A children's watch that always has the same time printed on its face could help rearrange your thoughts on time.

Little Books

The gigantic recovery movement has spawned a huge range of miniature books, filled with quotes and affirmations, arranged by the calendar day. Carrying a meditation book with you will nudge you to nurture yourself when your day gets tough.

Find a token *Little books*
Funny time

RESOURCES:

14,000 Things to Be Happy About, by Barbara Kipfer (Workman Publishing, 1990). Pick it up when you're down.

The Promise of a New Day: A Book of Daily Meditations, edited by Karen Casey (HarperSanFrancisco, 1996). One of the most powerful daily meditation books.

365 Travel: A Daily Book of Journeys, Meditations, and Adventures, edited by Lisa Bach (Travelers' Tales, 2001). For the traveler in you.

Meditations from the Mat: Daily Reflections on the Path of Yoga, by Rolf Gates and Katrina Kenison (Anchor, 2002). Centered on the practice of yoga.

Body, Mind, and Spirit: Daily Meditations, edited by Kristen Ison (Hazelden Educational Materials, 1995). Healing from addiction.

Coming Home to Myself: Daily Reflections for a Woman's Body and Soul, by Marion Woodman with Jill Mellick (Conari, 1998). Distillations of Woodman's wisdom!

Comfortable with Uncertainty: 108 Teachings, by Pema Chodron (Shambhala, 2002). Acorns of wisdom from her various books.

Pocketful of Miracles, by Joan Borenysko (Warner Books, 1994). Daily spiritual activities drawing from many wisdom traditions.

See "Creative Selfishness: Resources" and "Comfort Cards: Resources" for more titles.

Websites:

For the Little Ones Inside
http://www.forthelittleonesinside.com

Soulful Living
http://www.soulfulliving.com

Comfort Queen—Instant Soothing and Daily Dollop
http://www.comfortqueen.com

A FEW LAST THINGS

Self-nurturing is a lifetime commitment. It doesn't end when your life is going well or when you meet the partner of your dreams or get your fantasy job. Make comforting yourself part of your daily life, even when things are going your way. As women, we nurture life itself. We deserve to nurture ourselves as well.

You stand beside a calm pond. The setting sun lights up the landscape with shafts of purple and pink light. You toss a smooth pebble into the middle of the pond. Ripples radiate out until small waves lap at your feet. As the last rays of the sun disappear over the horizon, you realize by caring for yourself, you care for many, many others.

Please visit me at http://www.comfortqueen.com, and subscribe to my free e-zine newsletter, *The Self-Care Minder.* We are creating a lively, grace-filled, flaws-and-all global community of women who are exploring how to creatively, joyfully, fully live their lives. Be part of that community!

You can also reach me at P.O. Box 10065, Bainbridge Island, WA 98110.

May you be at peace.

ACKNOWLEDGMENTS

Thank you to the patient and intelligent women who gave me their time for interviews. A special thanks to Nancy Carter, Garry Diamond, Virginia Gilbert, Madelyn Hathaway, Rachelle Krupp, Hope Layton, Susanne Mentzer Landmesser, Lynn Martins, Judith Morse, Nina Luce, Miriam Rubinstein, Brenda Norman, Lois Carlton, Shelley Van Löben Sels, and Colby Smith. To Paula Steinmetz, you were an excellent resource throughout this project. Your support was a blessing.

My deep gratitude to the hundreds of women who responded to my questionnaire. Your replies inspired and guided me. Special thanks to Jibralta Merrill, Camille Thomasson, and Mahin Sanati.

Sara Lou O'Connor, thank you for your invaluable help editing the book proposal and for reading several drafts. Julie Kearney, Deborah Smith, and Nicole Smith, thanks for your insightful suggestions. Nicole Dillenberg, thanks for making me jealous. Zahra Dowlatabadi, your early support, unflagging enthusiasm, and ideas were priceless in keeping me going when I wanted to give up. Barbra Glascock Clifton, your enthusiasm for the book (and for me) is a precious gift. Beth, Michele, Mom, and Dad, your conviction as a family that I have something to say, and a good way to say it, makes me a very lucky woman. To Christopher Martin Mosio, your friendship, love, and passion for my work continue to carry me through my darkest hours.

And to Barbara Moulton, my superb editor, thank you for your calm, wise spirit and excellent ideas. I can't imagine a more relaxed, productive, comforting working relationship. Thanks to all the Harper folks for your help and ideas.

Thank you all so very much for enhancing this project.